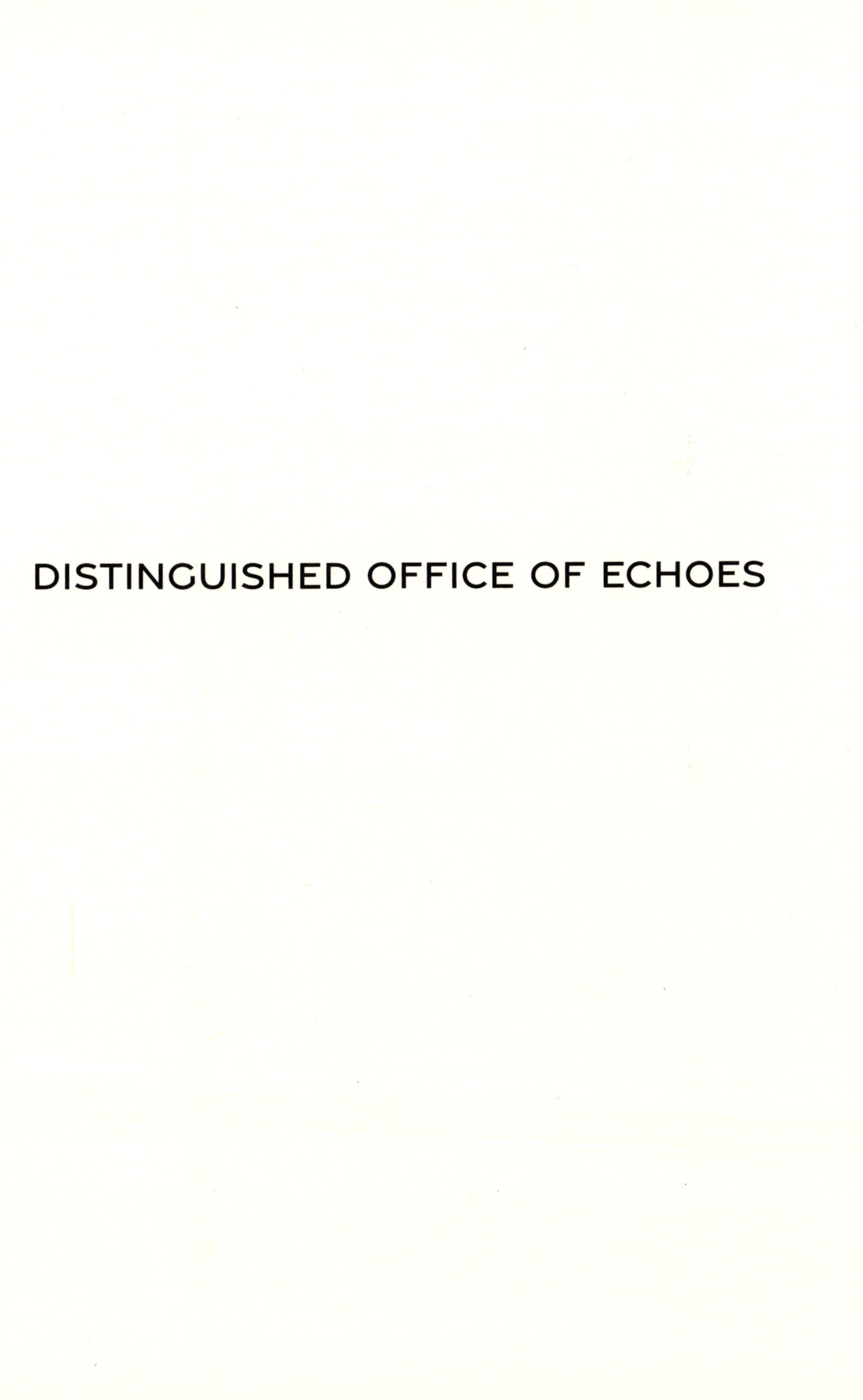

DISTINGUISHED OFFICE OF ECHOES

DISTINGUISHED OFFICE OF ECHOES

LISA OLSTEIN

COPPER CANYON PRESS

PORT TOWNSEND, WASHINGTON

INNER COAST

EFACE.

THIS volume is published with the hope of supplying a want often expressed

in order to

render it,

a complete picture of the type.

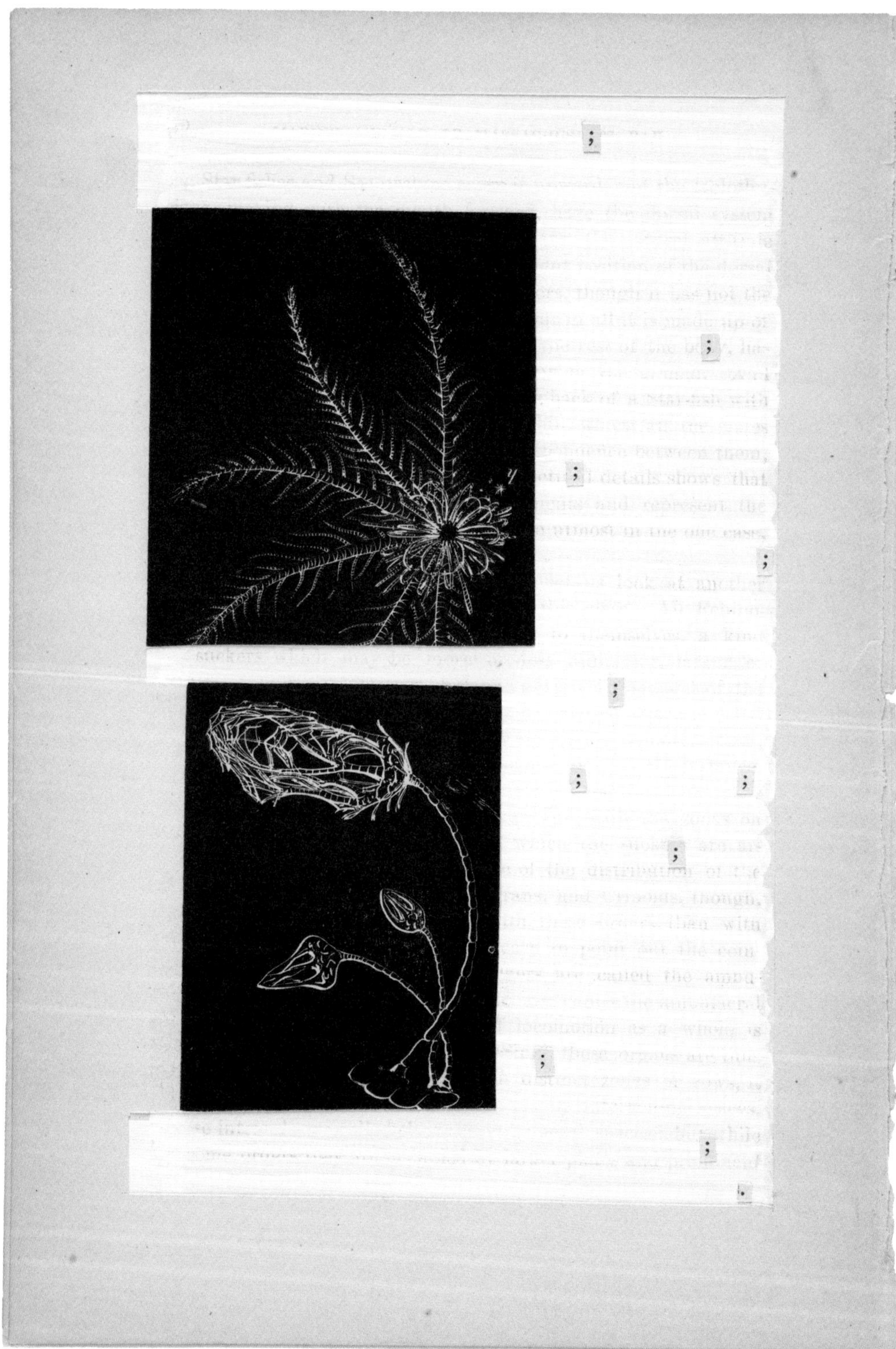

IT is perhaps not strange that

the investigation

once begun

should

become

here and there,

unravelled

the many
memoirs the great works

the admirable works

the objects of their study
all their
charming

investigations

the almost fabulous transformations

so
seemingly disconnected
we seem to have several where we have
but one.

Before

Fig. 1.

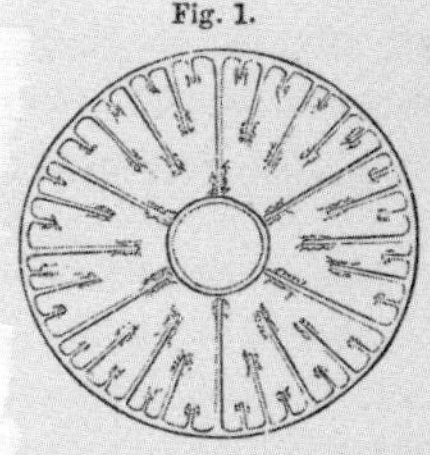

hanging

for example,

the body is fringed by hollow chambers.

These myriad whips

galvanic

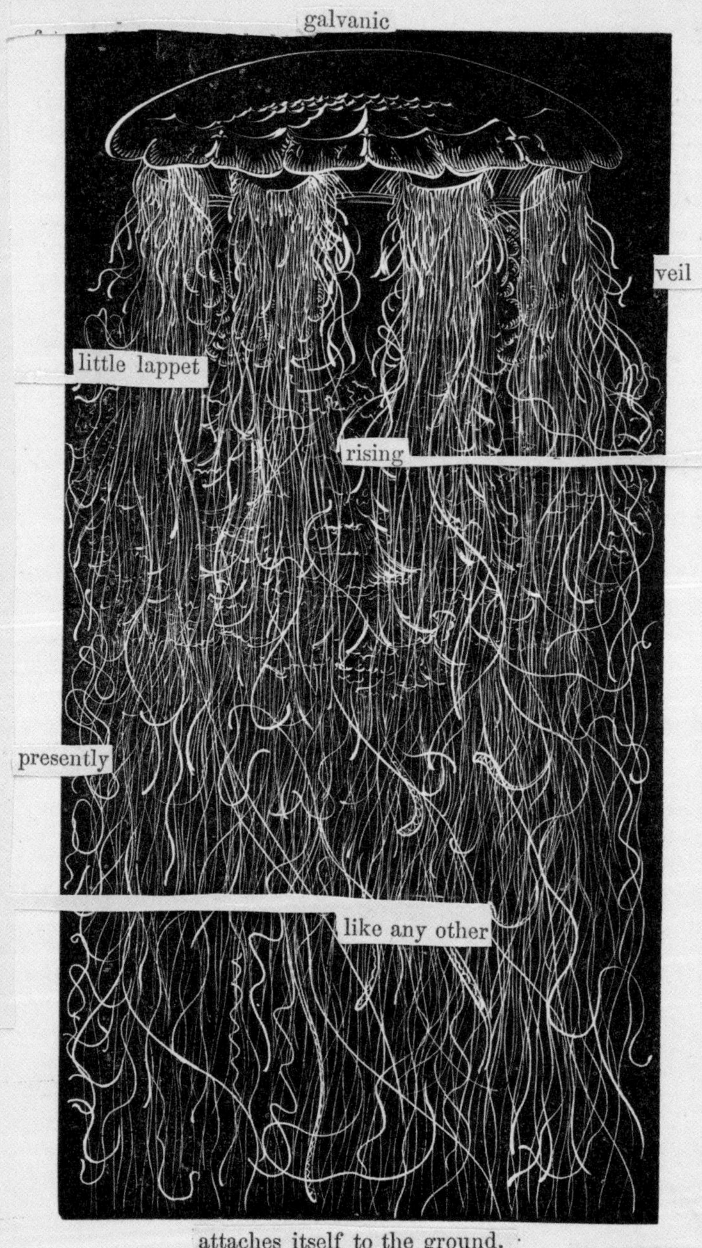

veil

little lappet

rising

presently

like any other

attaches itself to the ground.

pierced

ambulacrum

Fig. 131.

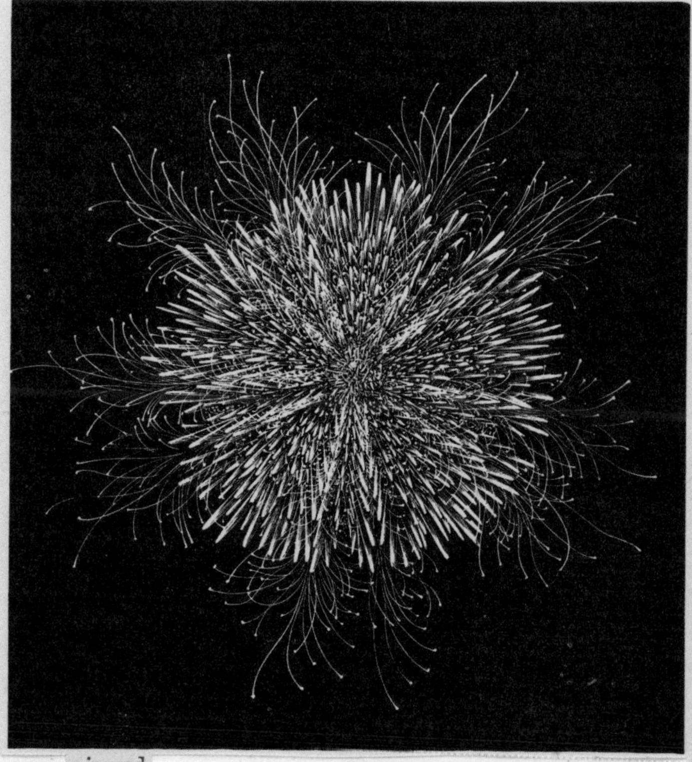

pierced

ambulacral

these teeth

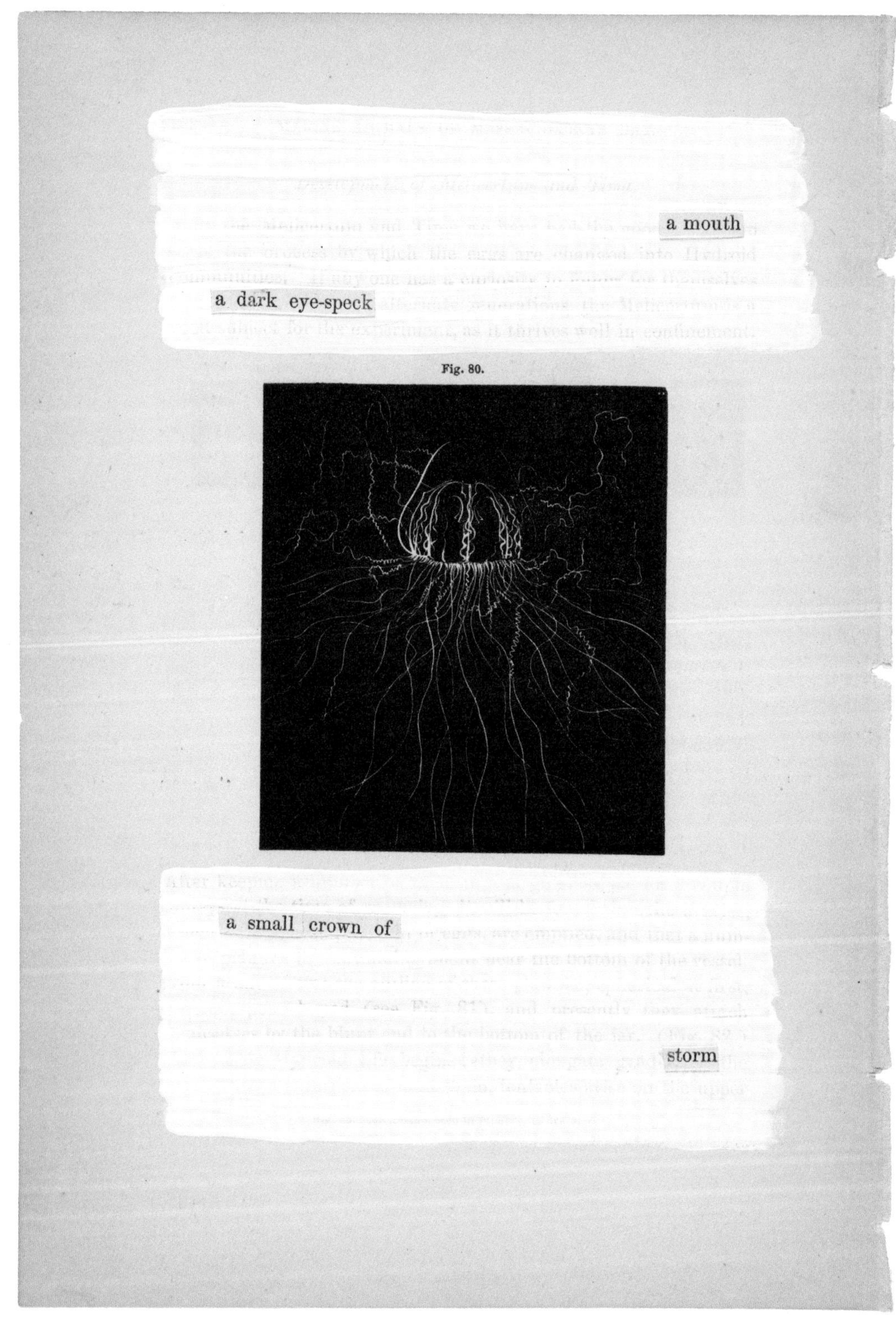
a mouth
a dark eye-speck
Fig. 80.
a small crown of
storm

slowly
hardly perceptible the body drops

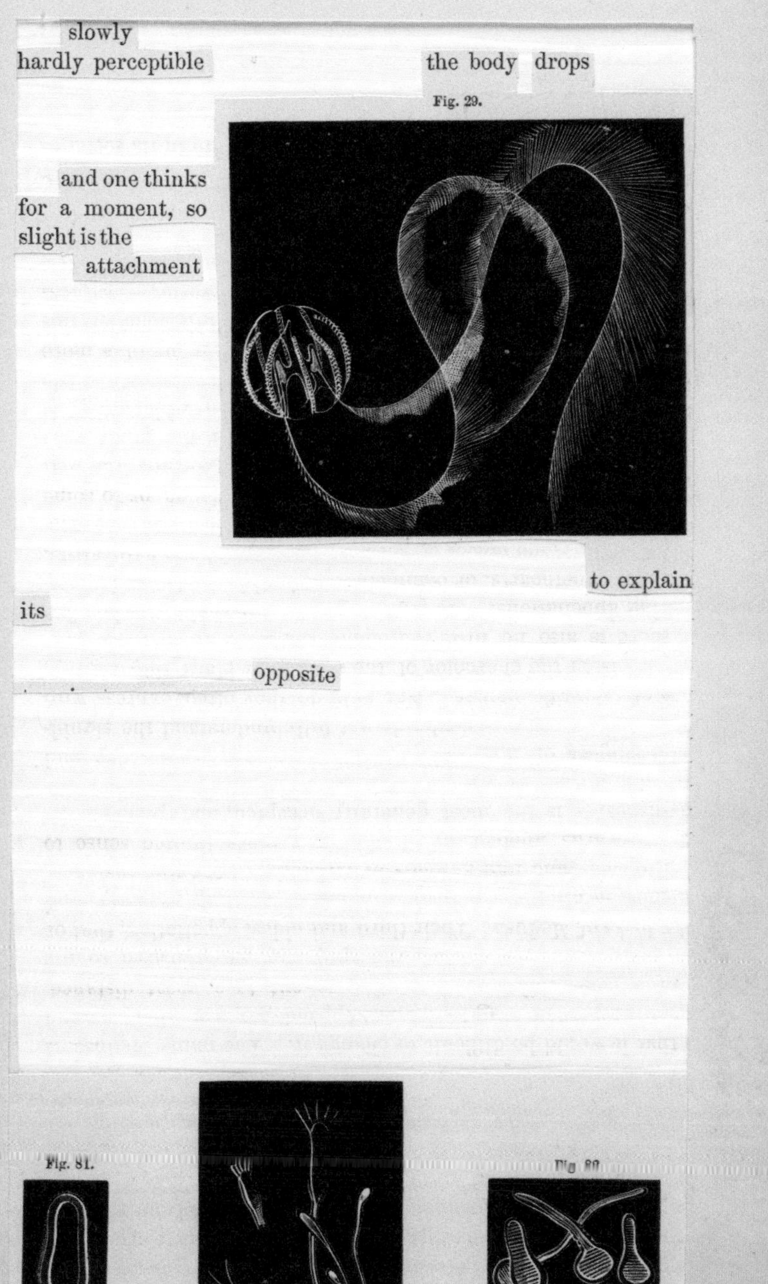

Fig. 29.

and one thinks
for a moment, so
slight is the
attachment

to explain
its

opposite

Fig. 81.

Fig. 80

We would say for the benefit of

the curious

one is
obliged to creep on hands and knees
through

that
roof
which is

completely hidden

but for the better explana-
tion the
body may be
described as a gelatinous bag

NOTHING can be more unprepossessing than

the flower after which it has been called.

now

its

vase is hollow

nevertheless

Fig. 55.

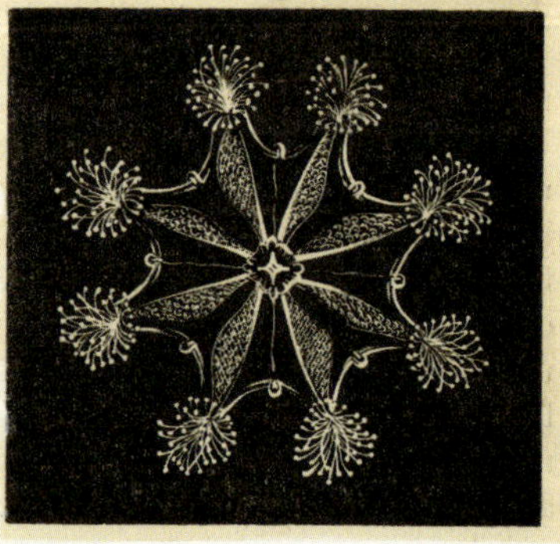

so

many

running

to

running from

EMBRYOLOGY OF CTENOPHORÆ.

ALL the Ctenophoræ are reproduced from eggs ; these eggs
are so transparent that one may follow with comparative ease
... by the young while still within the egg
... ely, however, they are so delicate that it is
... m alive for any length of time, even by
... antly with fresh sea-water, and keeping
... tion, both of which are essential conditions
... is therefore only from eggs accidentally
... ages of growth that we may hope to ascer-
... ing the sequence of their development.

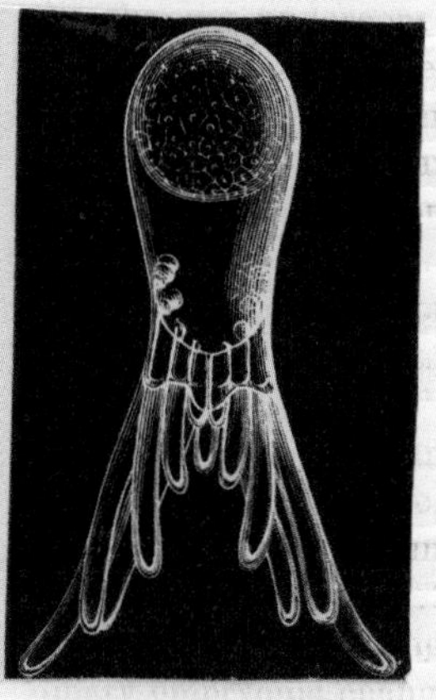

... ared with the size of the egg envelope, and
... e, it swims about with great velocity within
... nutive prison (Fig. 33). The ...
... better
... g the Ctenophoræ. Before their extraor-
dinary ... changes were understood, many of the young
... had found their way into our scientific annals as ; distinct
... nomenclature thus became burdened with
... which will disappear as our knowledge ad-

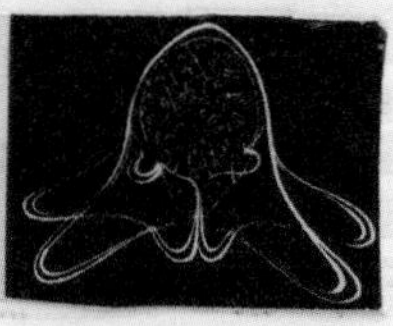

... their locomotive ; appers in proportion to the
... characteristic of the young Ctenophoræ.

parent spheres, and owing to their ... ;

... quickness of motion in after
...

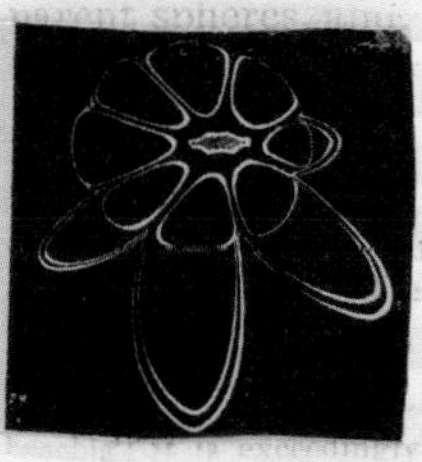

... the young (Fig. 34), ; t its active little body
... in the earlier stages of growth

... it is exceedingly flattened and pear-shaped. This species was discovered
long ago by Fabricius, but ... ;
(A. Agassiz.) .

Let us begin with its earlier condition. When it first escapes we may trace faint thread-like lines running from the summit

Fig. 176.

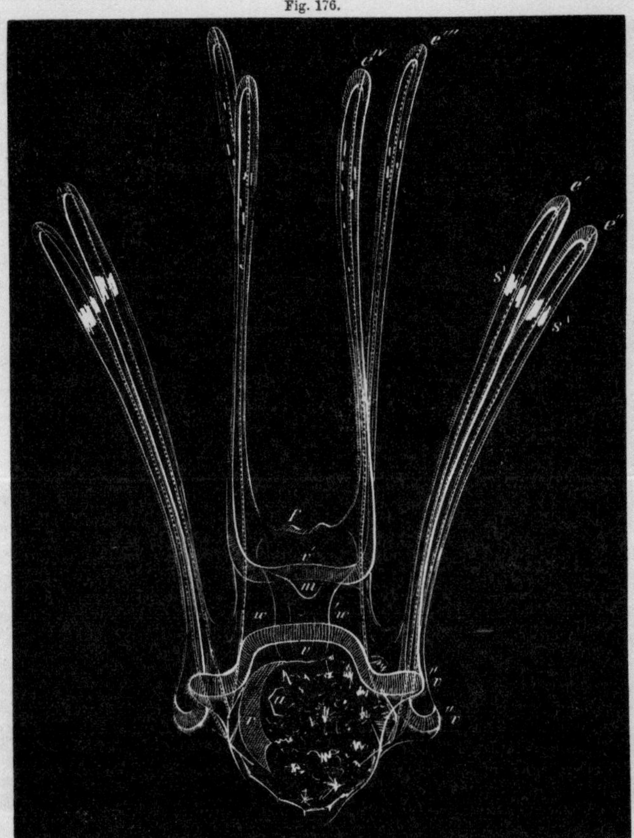

to the margin, where they meet. We may see the outline and we can detect the edge and we may perceive the filmy veil that fringes so delicate and unsubstantial, that with the naked eye the whole structure looks like and is a slight web of threads one perceives without being able to discern by what means they are held together. Under the mi-croscope, however, the invisible presently becomes visible, and we find that this is much to be regretted especially where it assumes a bell-shaped form, and is constantly spoken of as if it is.

Fig. 180.

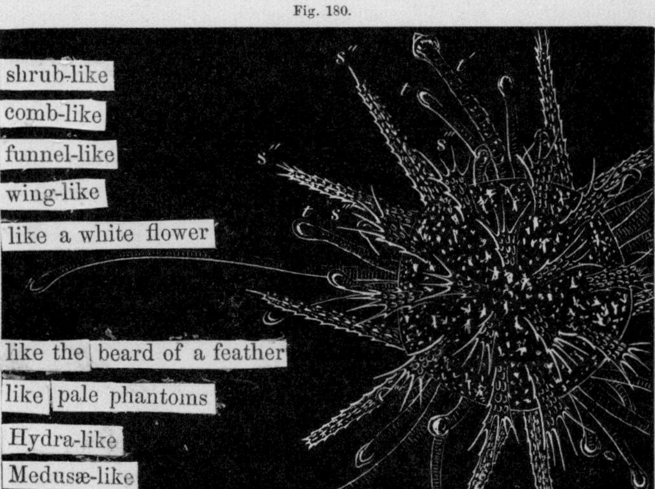

Fig. 181.

the swimming bells

are their oars

Fig. 115

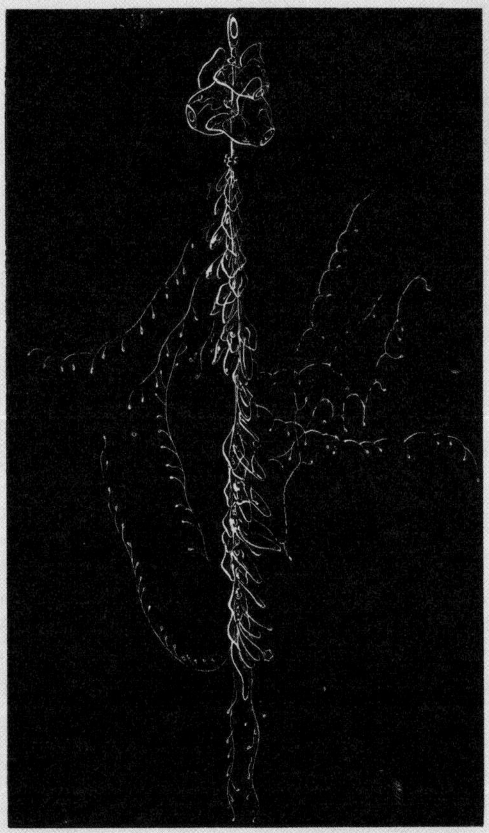

all the bells but first all the bells on
one side, and then all those on
the opposite

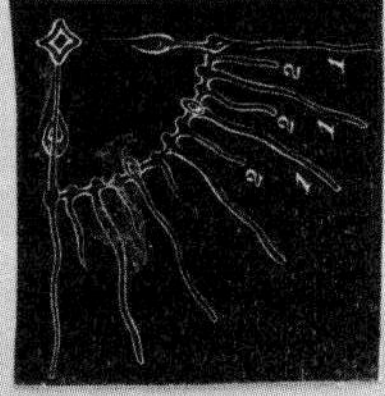

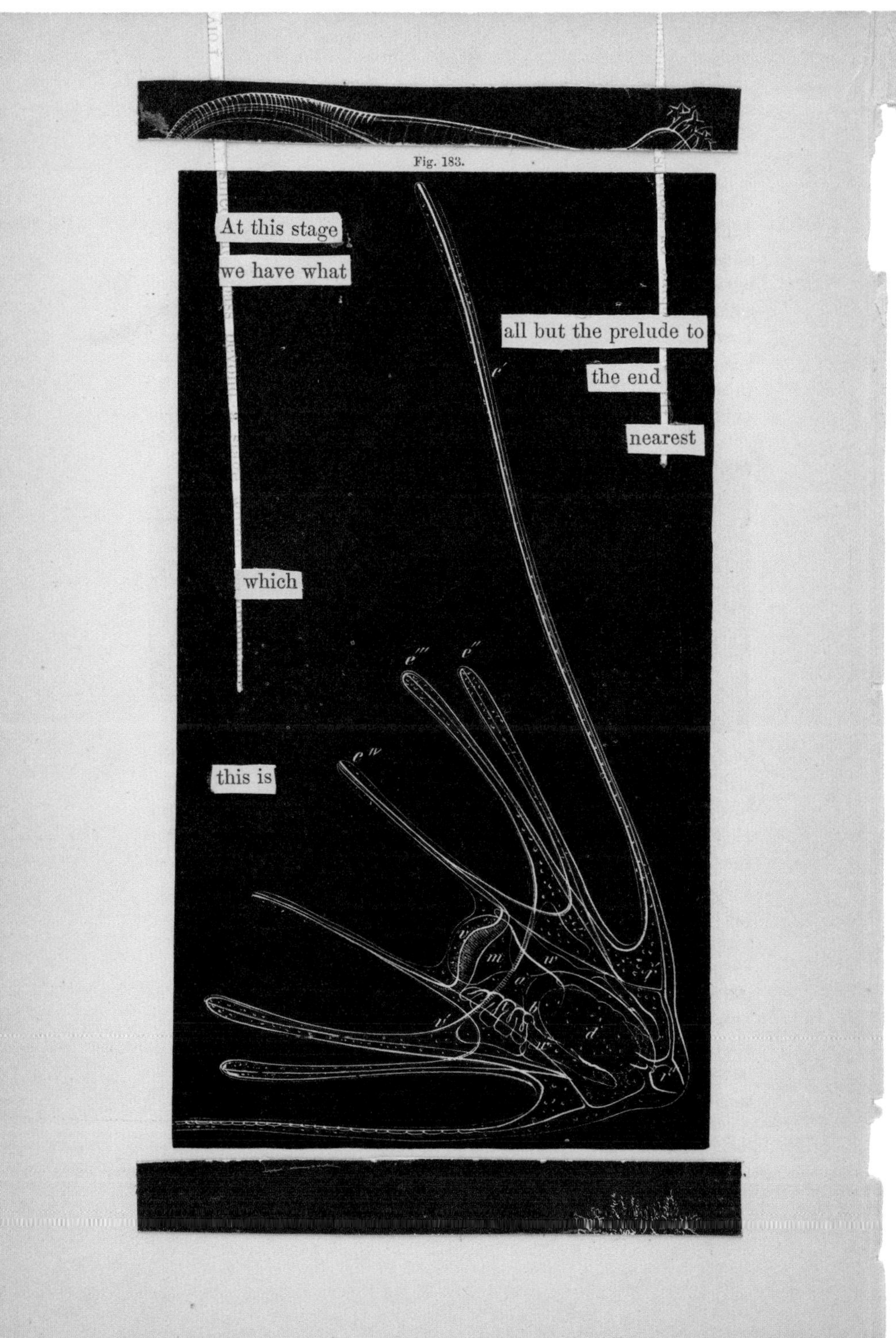
Fig. 183.
At this stage
we have what
all but the prelude to
the end
nearest
which
this is

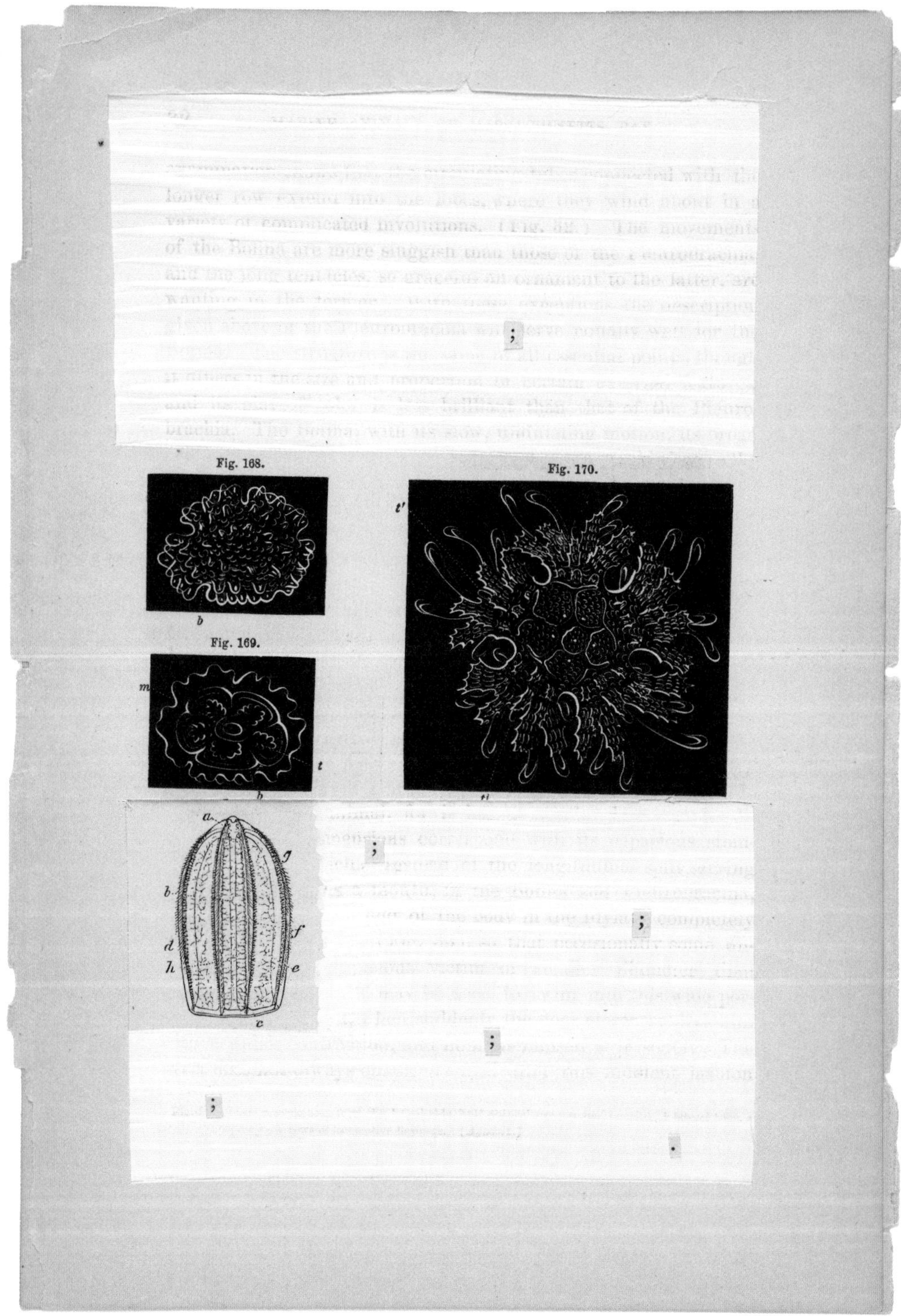

Fig. 168.
Fig. 169.
Fig. 170.

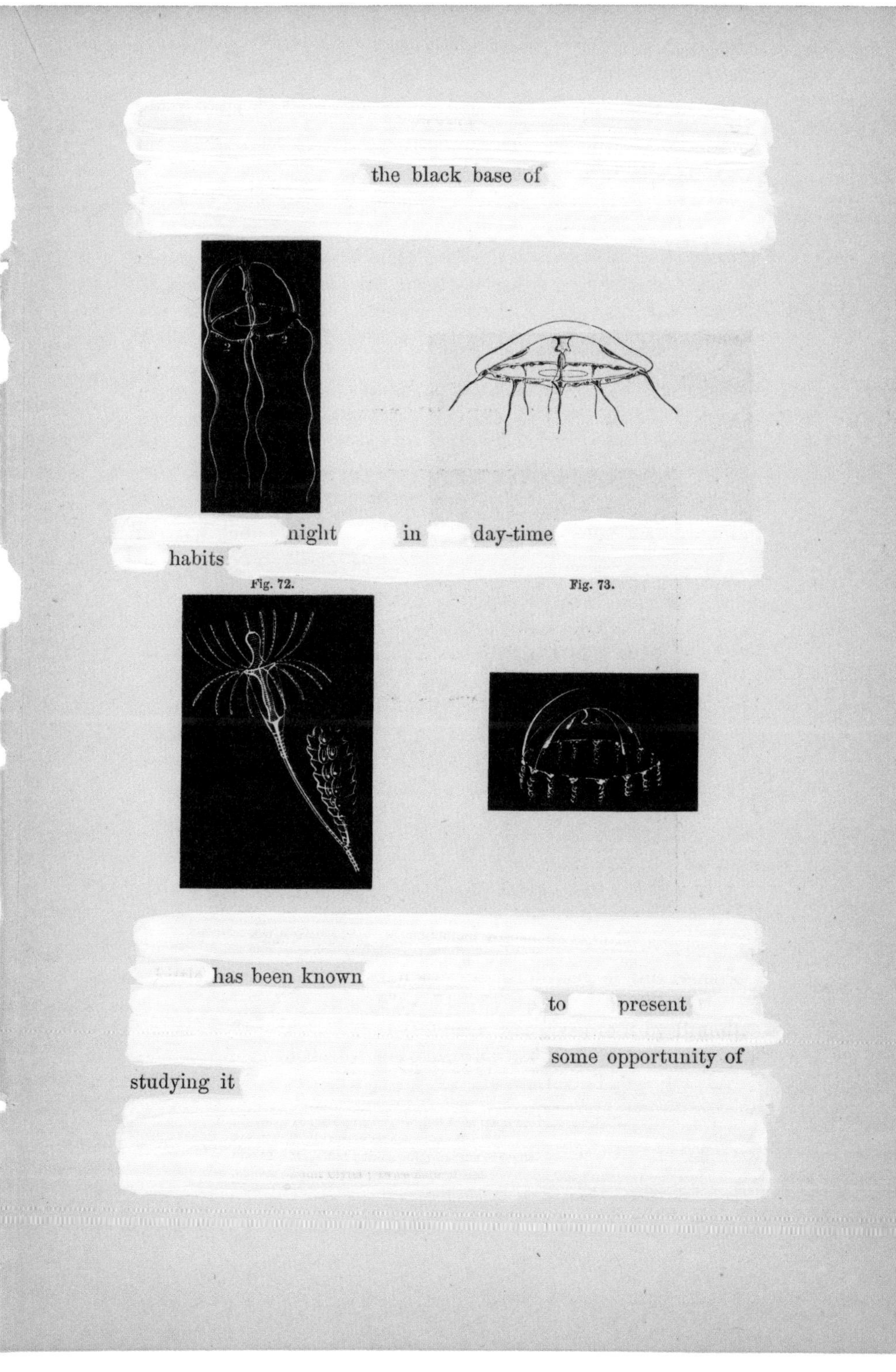

the black base of

night in day-time

habits

Fig. 72.

Fig. 73.

has been known

to present

some opportunity of

studying it

at the point where

like a flat blade

terminating in

Fig. 75.

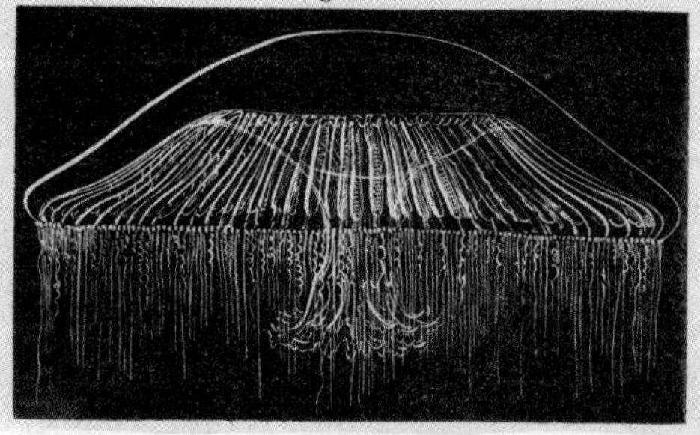

the mouth

a variety of names, likely to
mislead rather than aid have been ap-
plied to

that
which it encloses

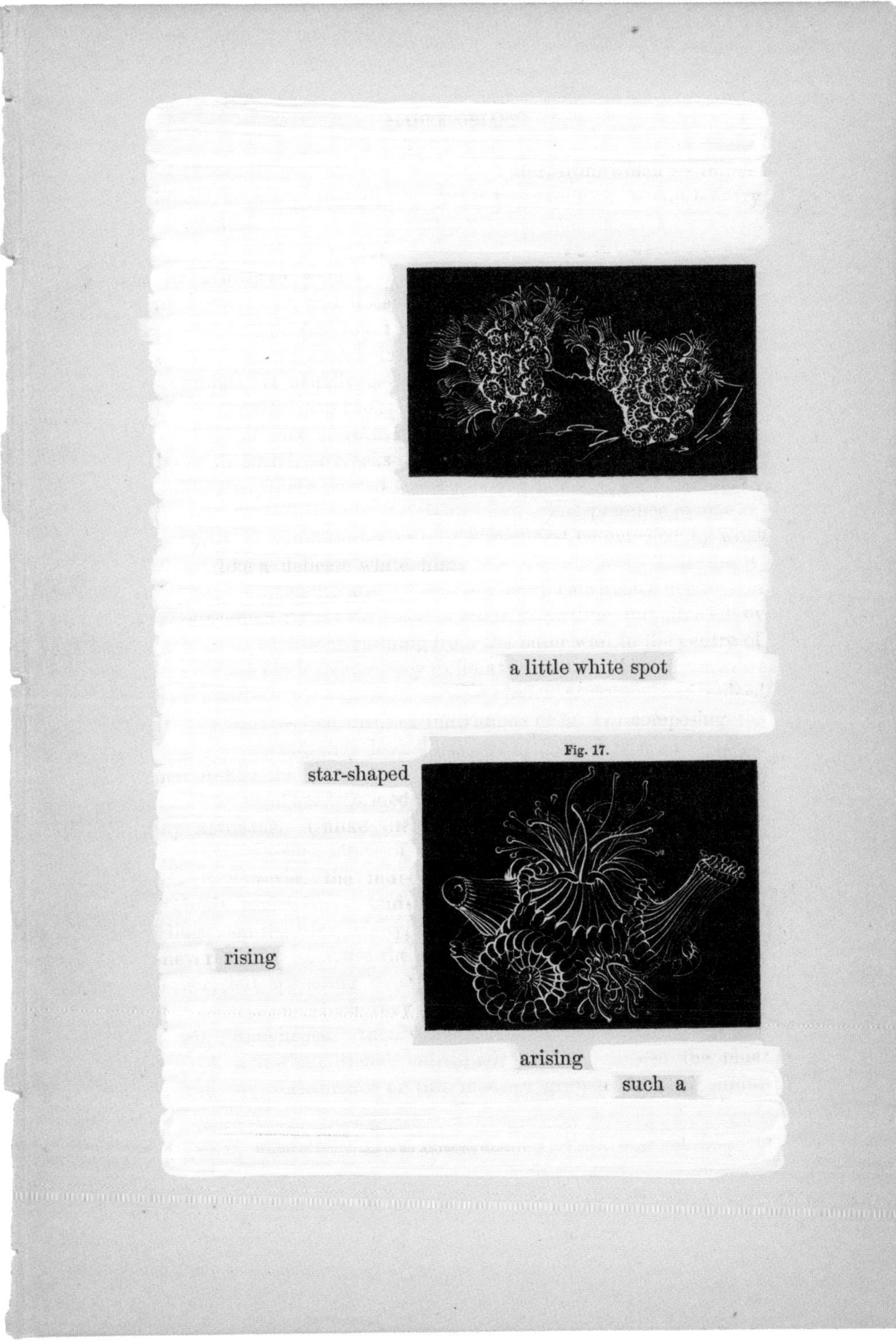
a little white spot
Fig. 17.
star-shaped
rising
arising
such a

beautiful floating Medusa
heart-shaped open-mouthed
ever-gaping Medusa

fixed or floating
budding, arising as buds
perfect Medusæ, hanging

floating swimming Medusæ
a colony of swimming bells
ordinary Medusæ, remember,

a singular hermit Medusa
superfluous like one animal
one primitive Medusa

a portion of

Medusæ

Fig. 124.

little flat boat with an upright sail
stranded
so far from their home

Fig. 142.

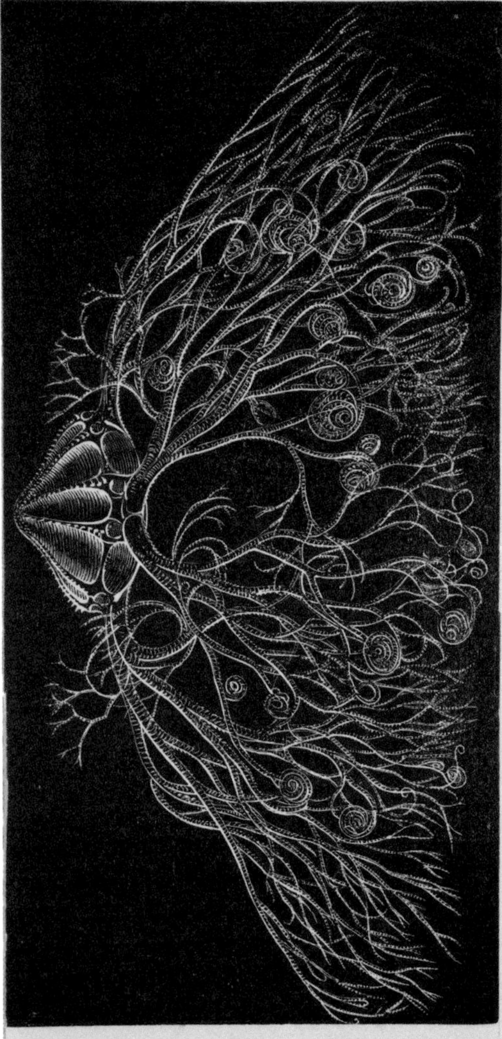

Fig. 151.

Nature has her culminating hours
Notwithstanding the beauty of
a moonlight row, you must choose a
dark night, when the motion of
your boat sets the sea on fire
around you   Now dip the net
and as the air rushes out
the water rushes in, and
our dirty, torn old net is sud-
denly turned to a web of gold
just the animal you want
when the clouds are so
thick that water, sky, and land
become one indiscriminate mass
of black, and one seems to be
rocking above a volcano
very different, when seen from
the deck of a vessel, from its
appearance as one floats
through its midst

it is a curious fact

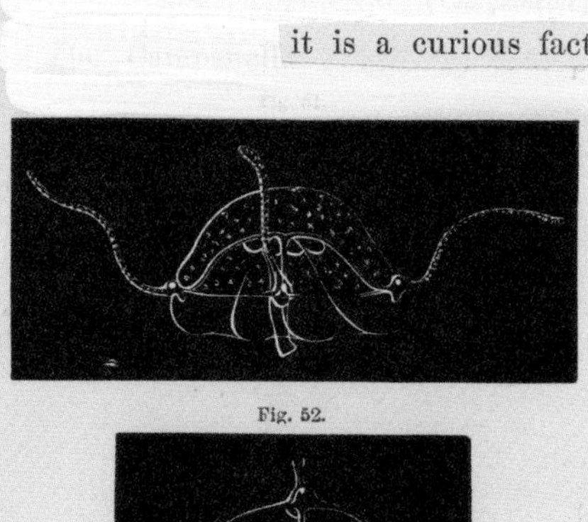

Fig. 52.

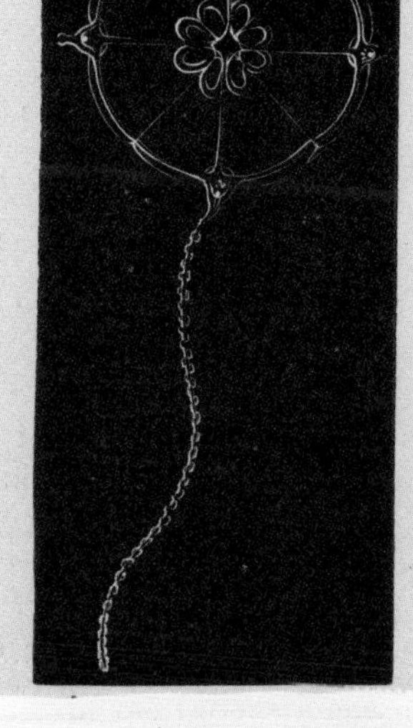

your oar as you lift it

its effect

see

the sea has

tiny lamps

little shining spheres

a long undulating wave

that dim spreading halo

the little creature you are trying to catch

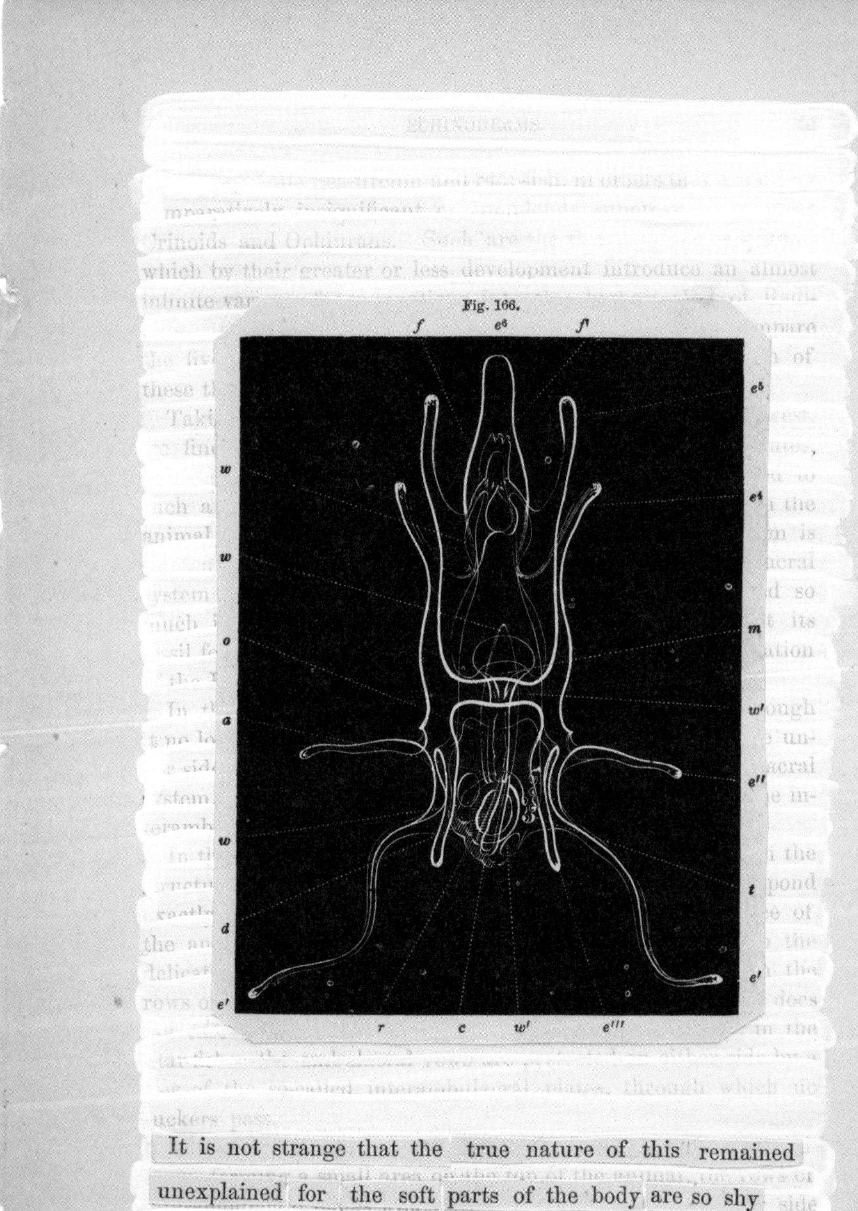

Fig. 166.

It is not strange that the true nature of this remained
unexplained for the soft parts of the body are so shy
of approach it is not easy to examine the living

The same is true of any stony beach or
rocky shore
Fig. 92.
Fig. 93.
of
great rivers haunted
of the woods,
of elms,
walnuts, beeches, birches, maples,
birds
buffaloes, bears, wolves, foxes,
deer

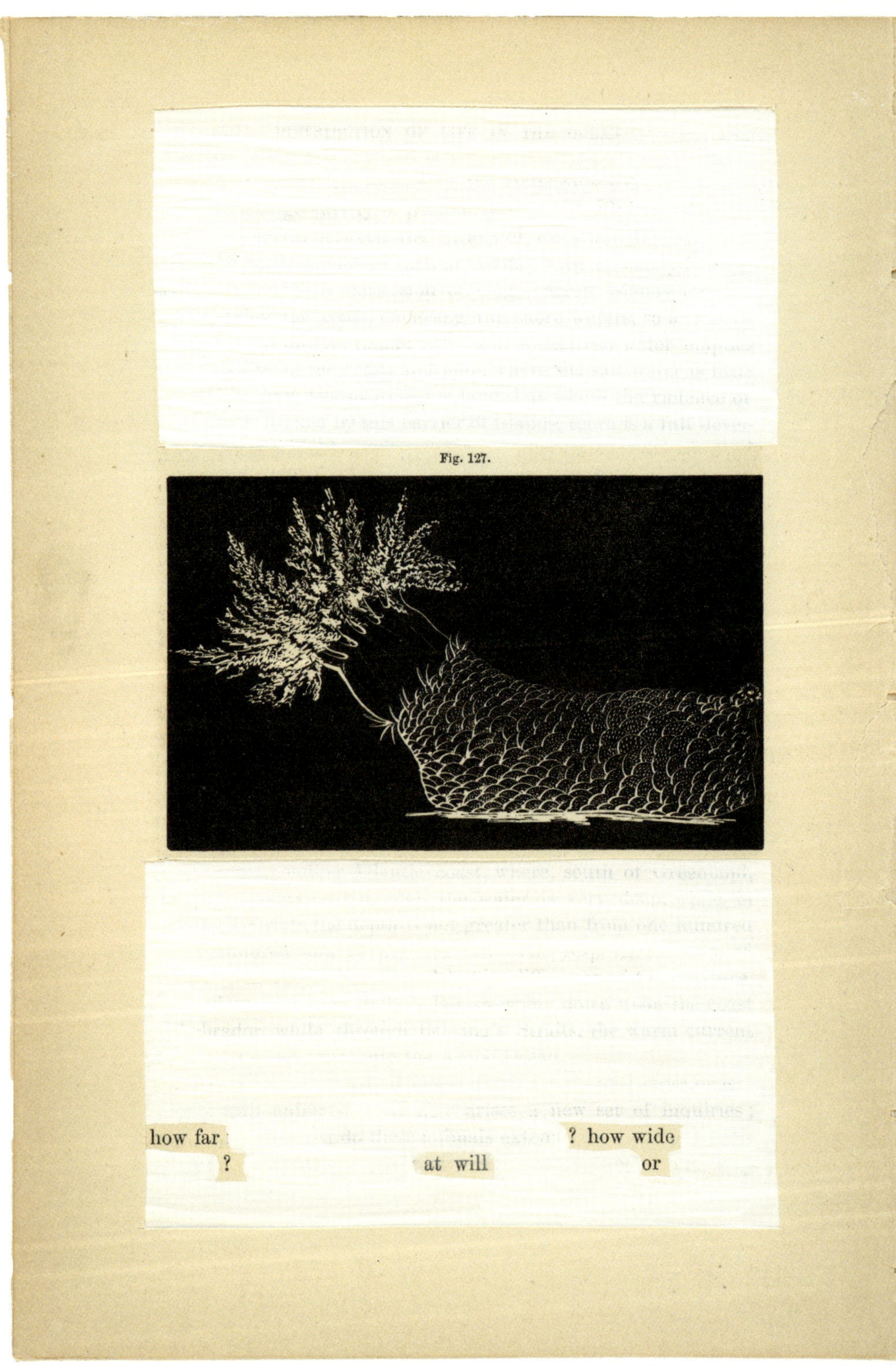

Fig. 127.

how far ? how wide

? at will or

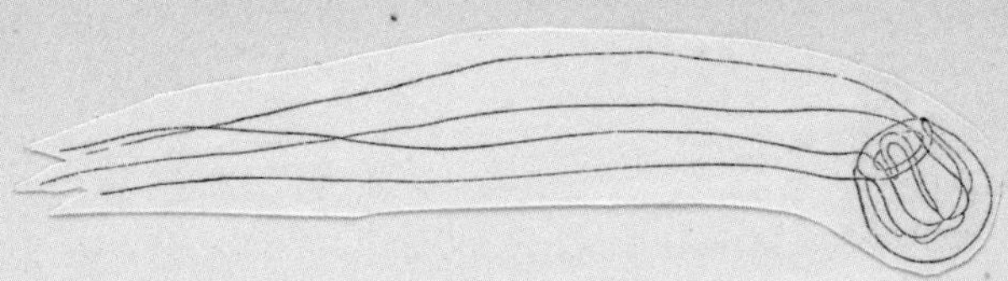

We will suppose it to be warm
at last

the horizon dim

The sea glassy

&c.

Now we are crossing the shallows

— how lovely

the long blades of

the tide rising,
laden with treasures

—

Here he is floating close by
now he is within the circle of the net

Fig 139.

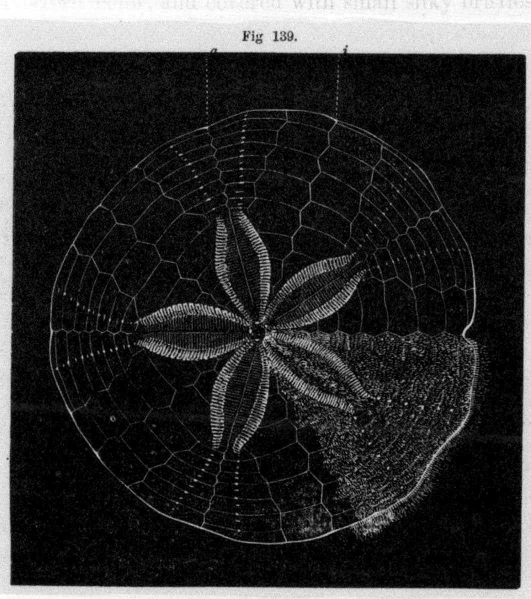

Sea- Sea-

Sea-

Fig. 147.
Star-
Star-
Star-

Fig. 148.

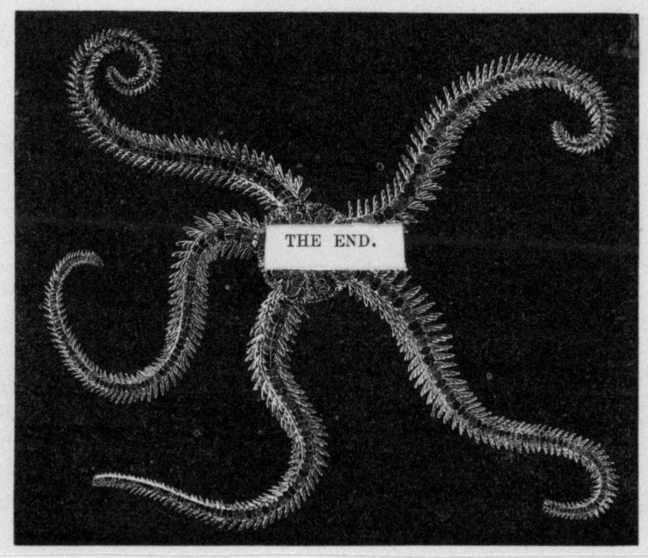

WAR WITH

in this little book

the heroes are not

some

girls who love the past

long ago,
there lived islands and
shores

little

fragments

the sea
rose and fell, and

lines
of animals and men

not
kingdom but collection

bound together
by

a friendly feeling between

oceans

their songs

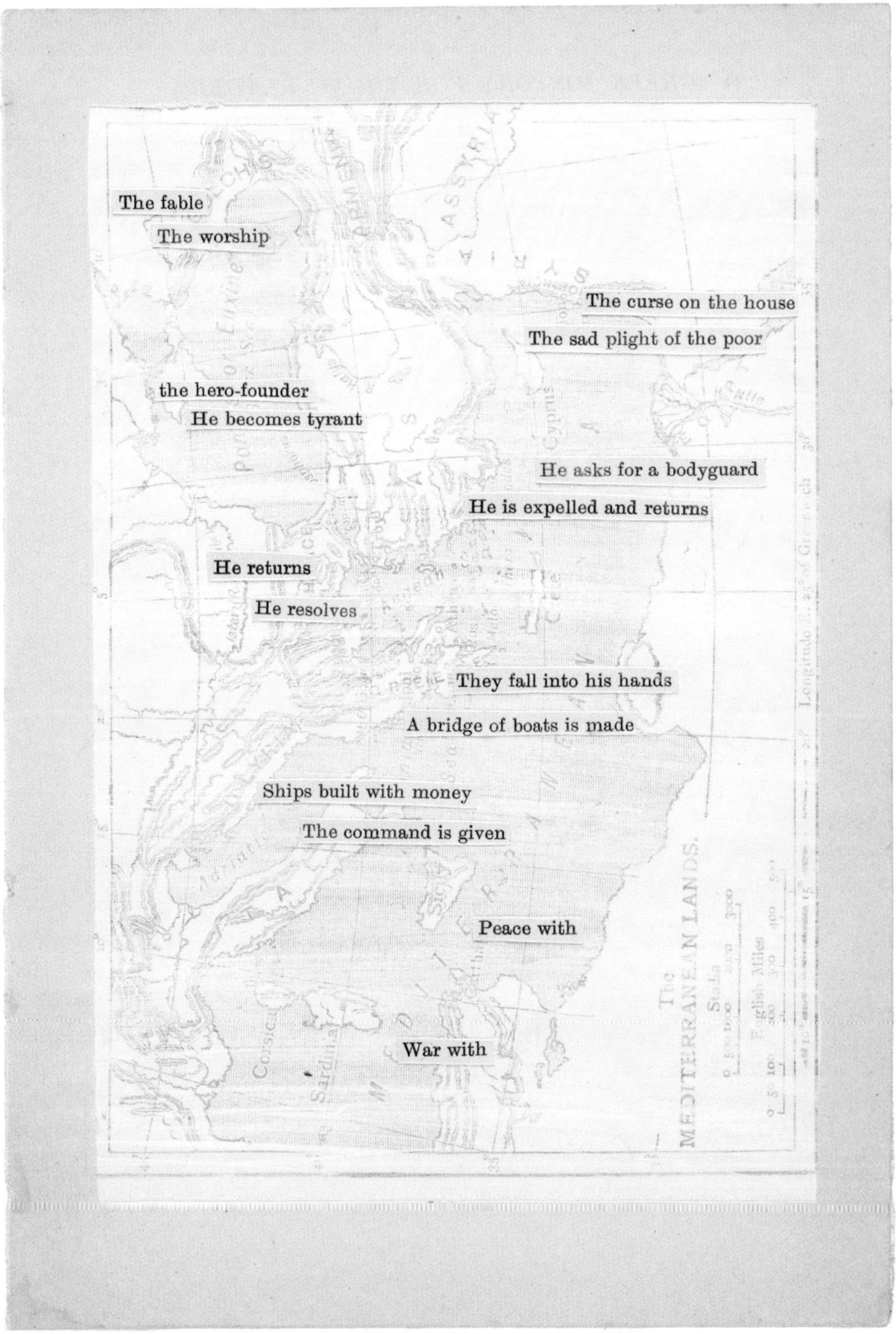

The fable

The worship

The curse on the house

The sad plight of the poor

the hero-founder

He becomes tyrant

He asks for a bodyguard

He is expelled and returns

He returns

He resolves

They fall into his hands

A bridge of boats is made

Ships built with money

The command is given

Peace with

War with

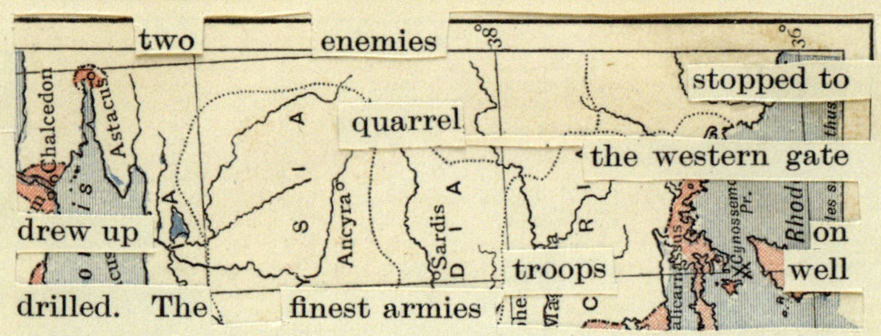
two
enemies
stopped to
quarrel
the western gate
drew up
on
troops
well
drilled. The
finest armies

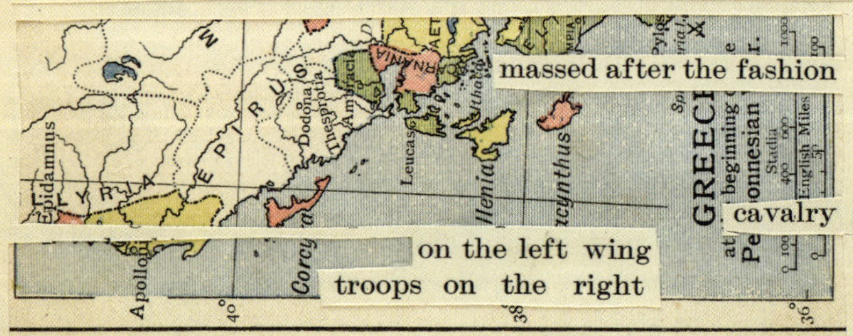
massed after the fashion
cavalry
on the left wing
troops on the right

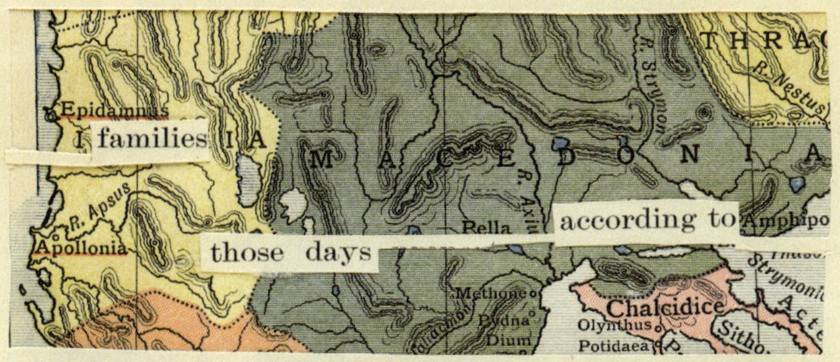

families

according to

those days

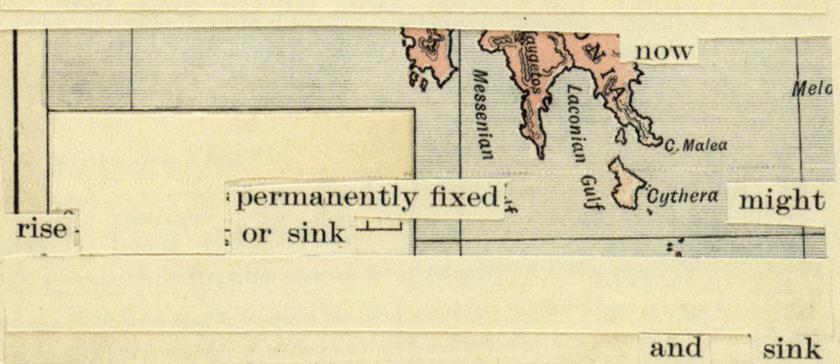

now

permanently fixed might

rise or sink

and sink

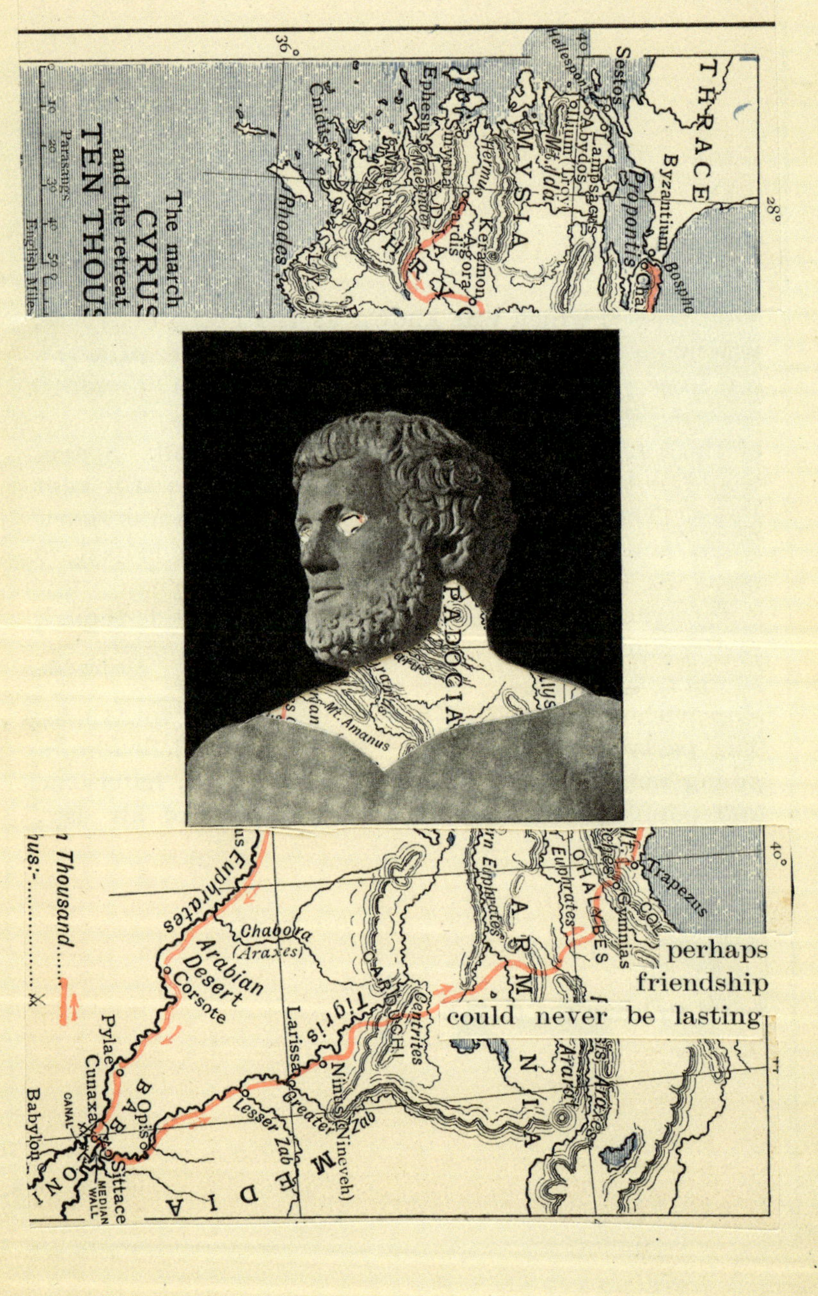
perhaps
friendship
could never be lasting

uncertain whether to sail further

or rest

your ships

will

beseech you deliver us.

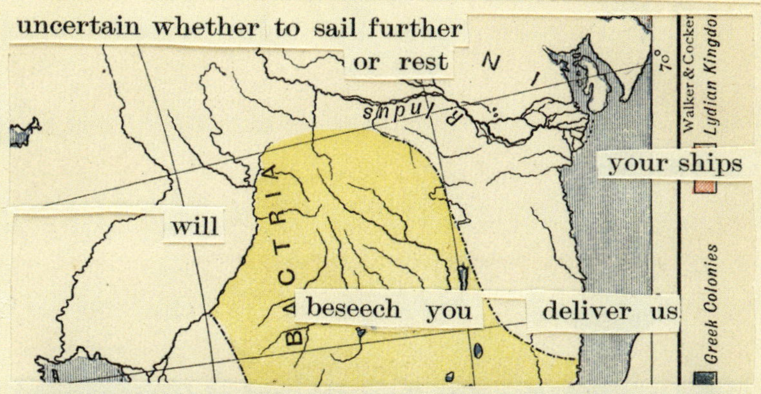

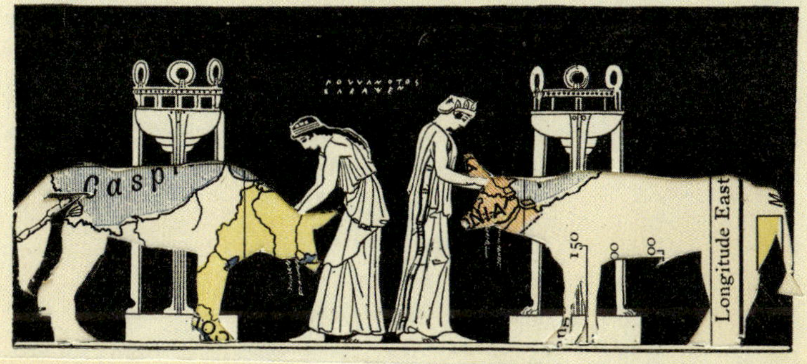

and we will go

return home prepare

not to risk a second

At sea

shelter,
R. Strymon
T H R A C E
CEDONIA
R. Hebrus
seemed to be
Doriscus
wherever
Sestos
Abydo
Troy
the battle was
At last
hope
panic
flight
never stop
run-
ning
C R E T E
Cnossos
Route of Xerxes
Fleet
24°

Nor had the part played by PHOCIS

been

the part played in

War sided with

after

changed

sides, and was first

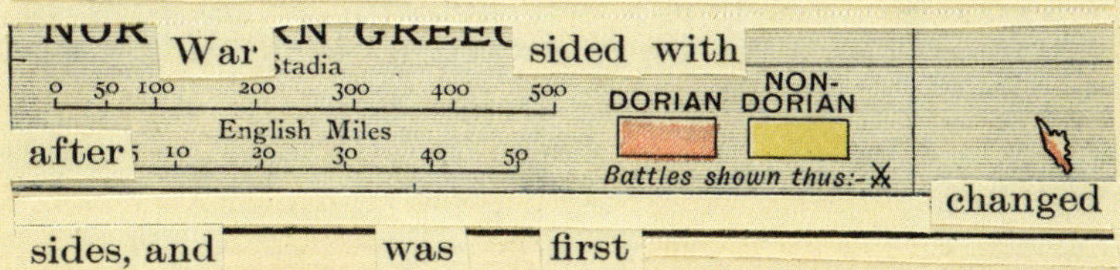

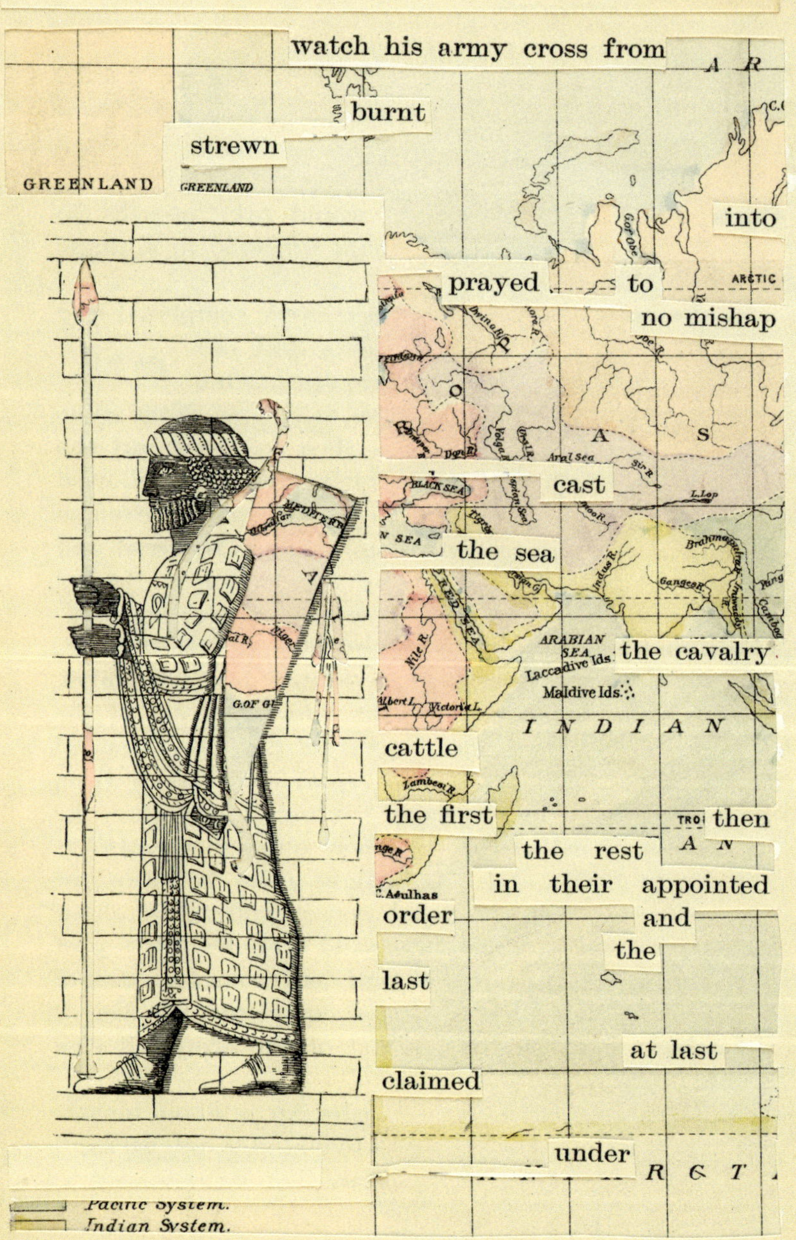
watch his army cross from
burnt
strewn
GREENLAND
into
prayed to
no mishap
cast
the sea
the cavalry
ARABIAN SEA
Laccadive Ids.
Maldive Ids.
INDIAN
cattle
the first
then
the rest
in their appointed
order
and
the
last
at last
claimed
under
Pacific System.
Indian System.

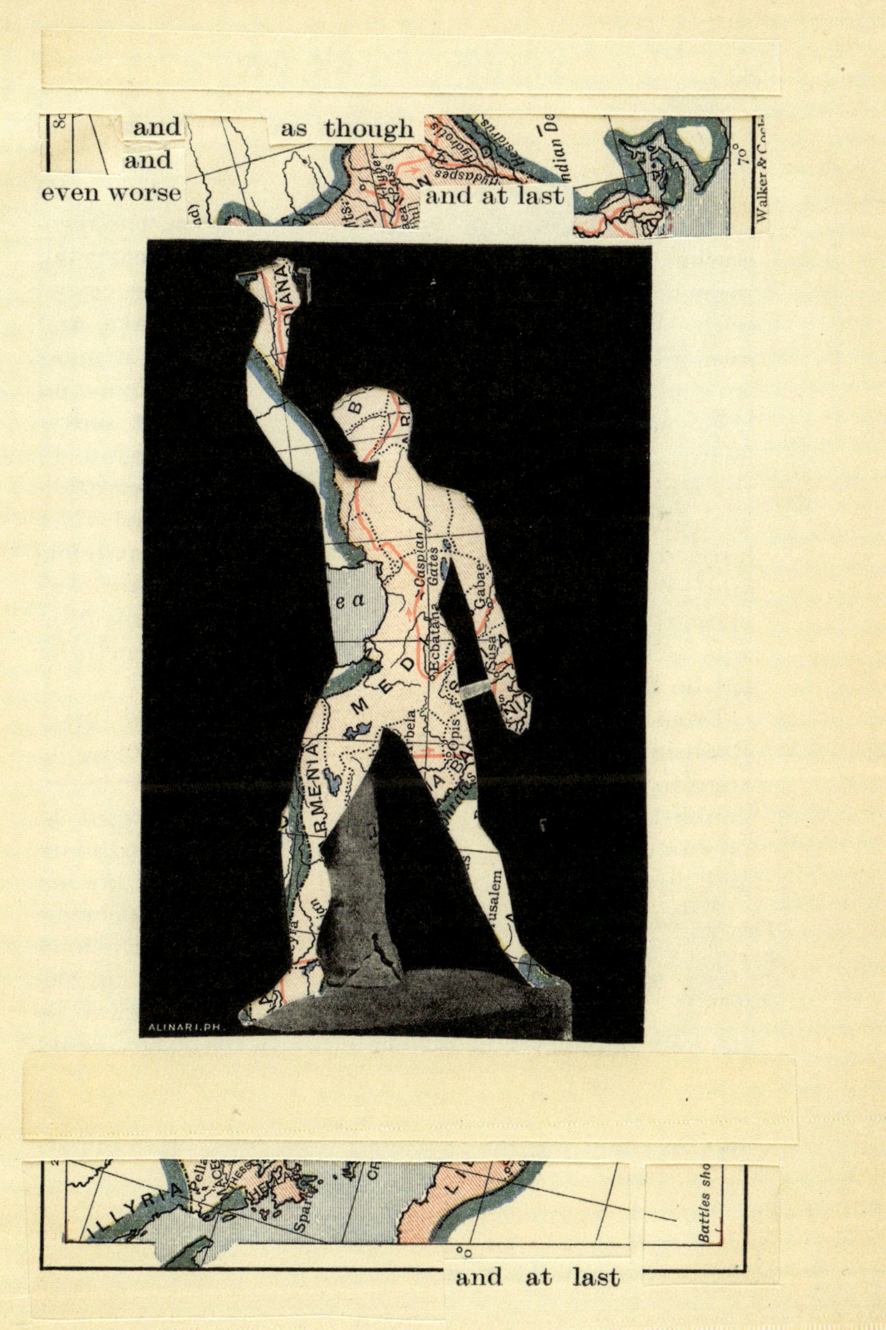
and
as though
and
even worse
and at last
and at last

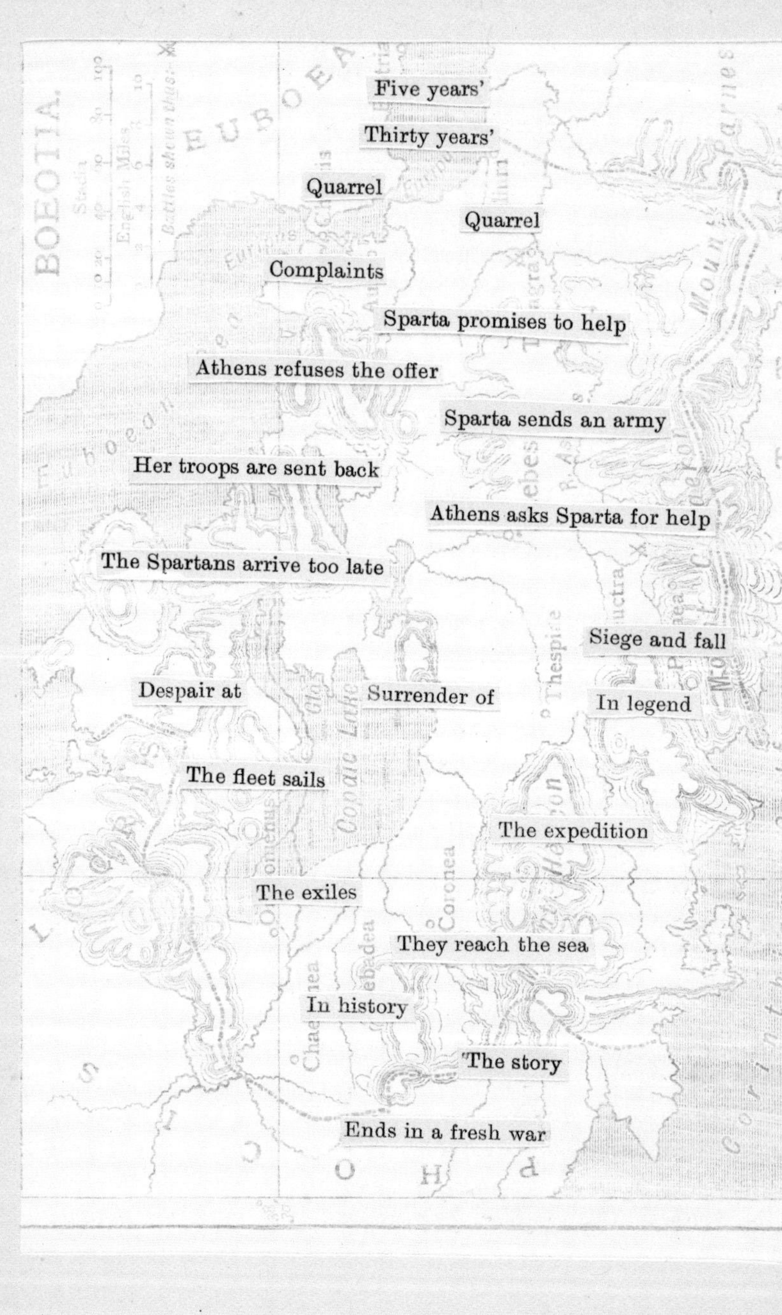
BOEOTIA.
EUBOEA
Five years'
Thirty years'
Quarrel
Quarrel
Complaints
Sparta promises to help
Athens refuses the offer
Sparta sends an army
Her troops are sent back
Athens asks Sparta for help
The Spartans arrive too late
Siege and fall
Despair at
Surrender of
In legend
The fleet sails
Copaic Lake
The expedition
The exiles
Coronea
They reach the sea
In history
The story
Ends in a fresh war
Mount Parnes

lovingly

the river

pours its waters into
the sea

of which we
know very little

no one
passing through

to tell us anything

in

the old
days,

who

slew the
lion

was home in their eyes

shepherd
of

hope and dream

but they

found he could not

work miracles after all

any

worth their while

little

monarch

subject to
so vast an empire.

of

rivers

ill-fated King

rivers deliver

the most wonderful

walls

at last a

promise

an empire too good
to throw away

NEAR AND DISTANT REGIONS

Shall we open our rooms to the night air?

The

hours

a cluster of geranium flow-

ers

breathing

snakes

Here the
air

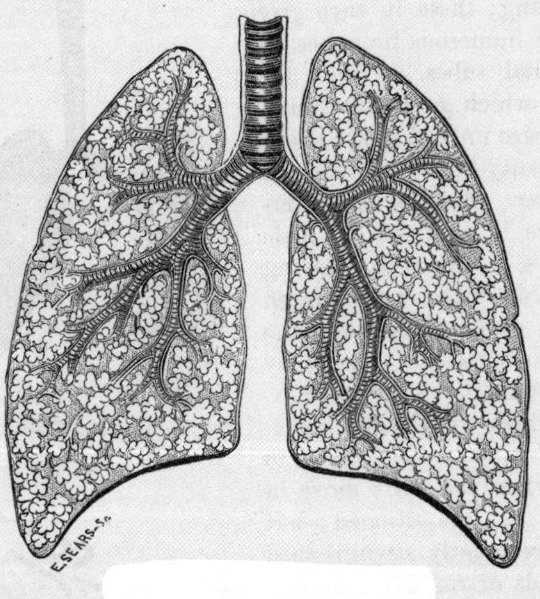

fits like the lid of a box
and closes
. Occasionally it does not close in time
and we
discover something has
gone wrong -
unwelcome intruder.

Now the

approach of disease calls

according to its want

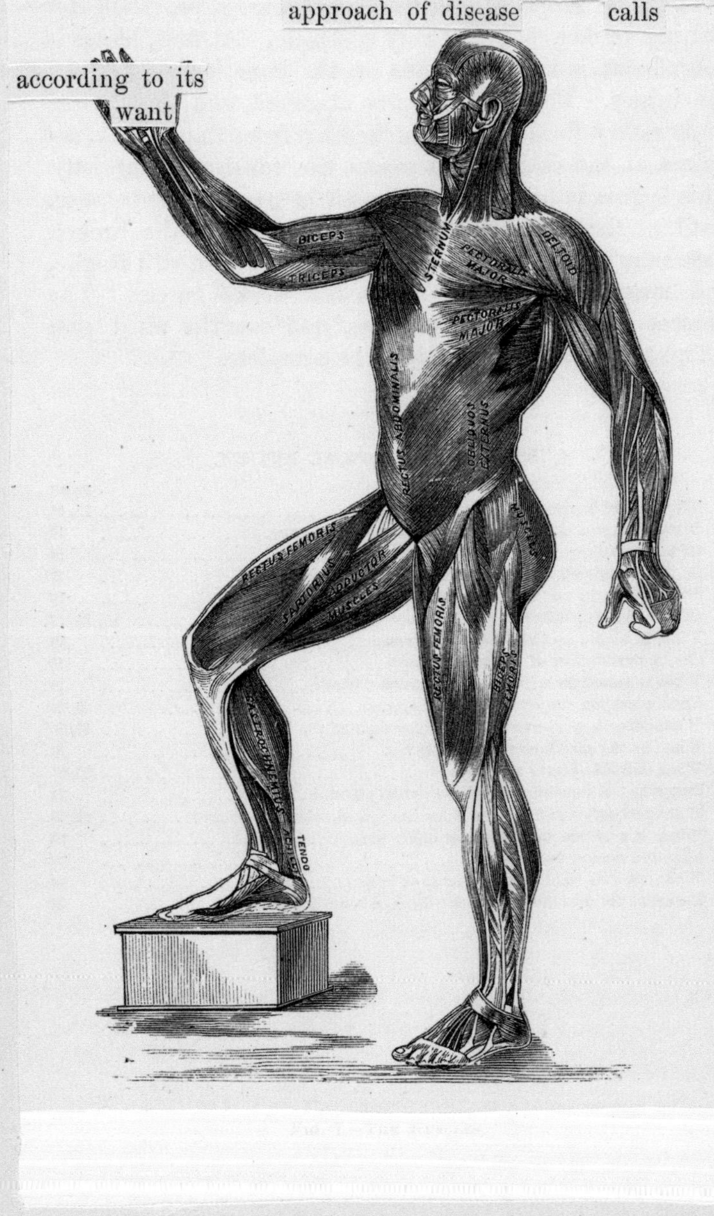

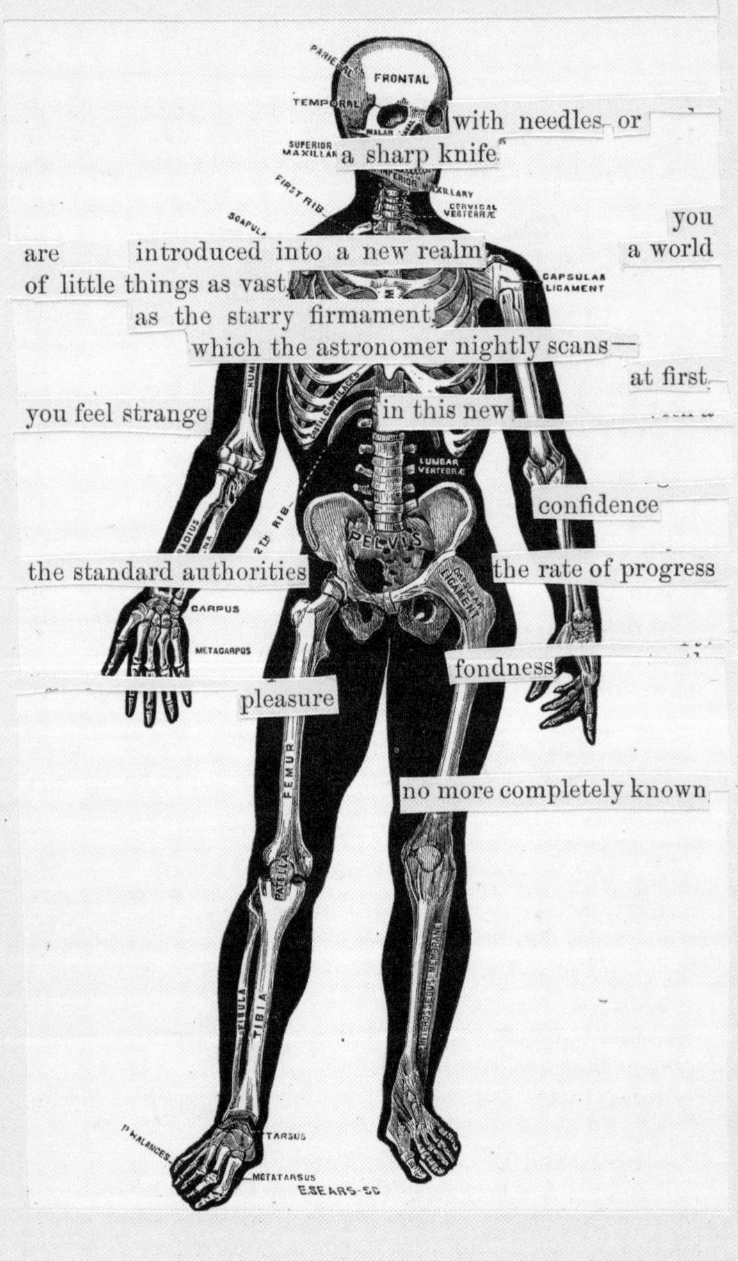
with needles or
a sharp knife
you
are introduced into a new realm a world
of little things as vast
as the starry firmament
which the astronomer nightly scans—
at first
you feel strange in this new
confidence
the standard authorities the rate of progress
fondness
pleasure
no more completely known
FRONTAL
TEMPORAL
SUPERIOR MAXILLARY
FIRST RIB
CERVICAL VERTEBRÆ
CAPSULAR LIGAMENT
LUMBAR VERTEBRÆ
PELVIS
CAPSULAR LIGAMENT
CARPUS
METACARPUS
FEMUR
PATELLA
FIBULA
TIBIA
TARSUS
METATARSUS
E.SEARS-SC

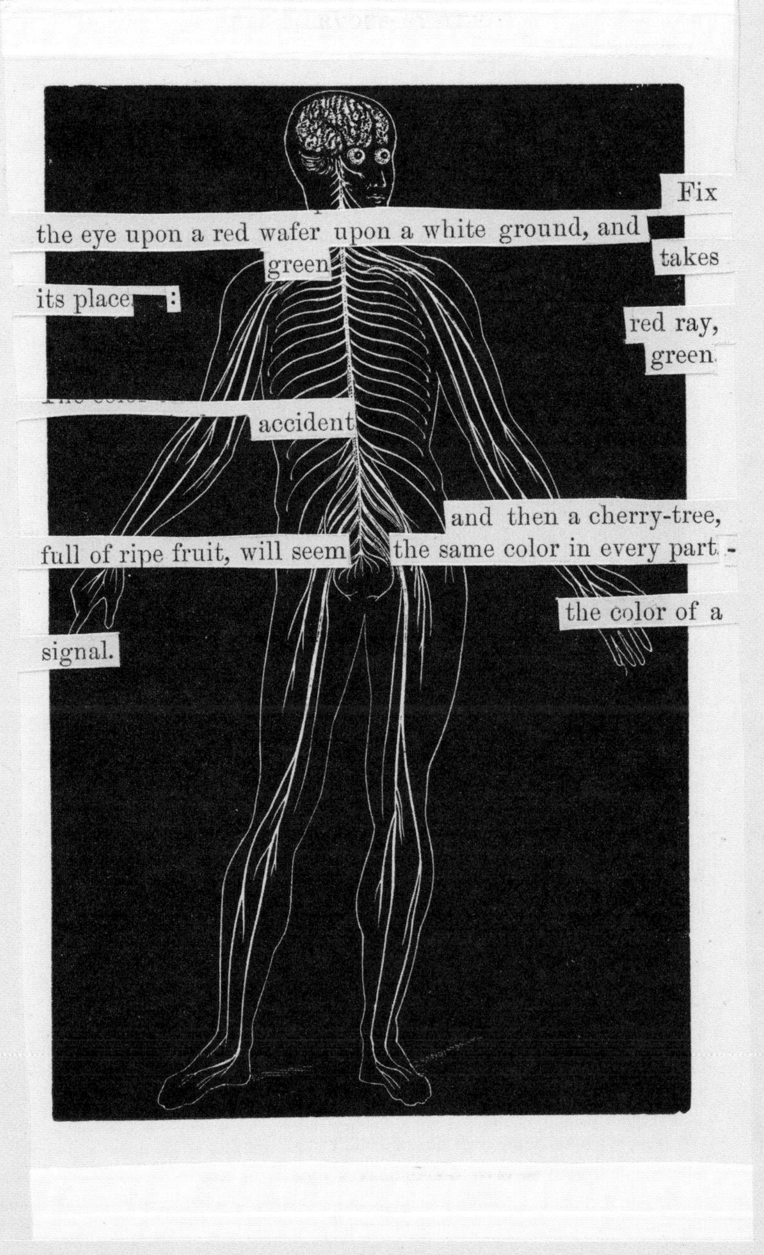
Fix
the eye upon a red wafer upon a white ground, and
green
takes
its place :
red ray,
green
accident
and then a cherry-tree,
full of ripe fruit, will seem the same color in every part -
the color of a
signal.

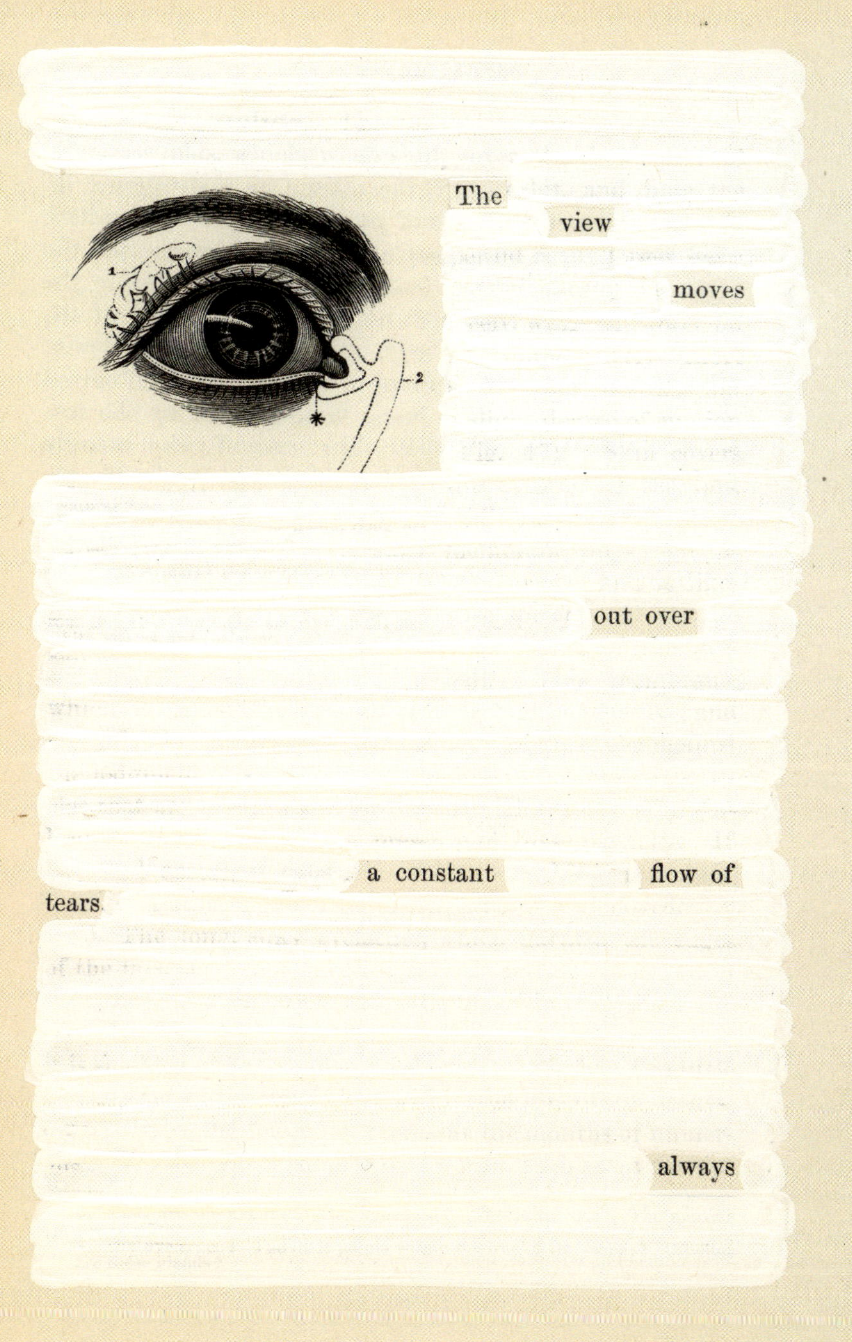
The
view
moves
out over
a constant flow of
tears
always

adjusting itself to distances

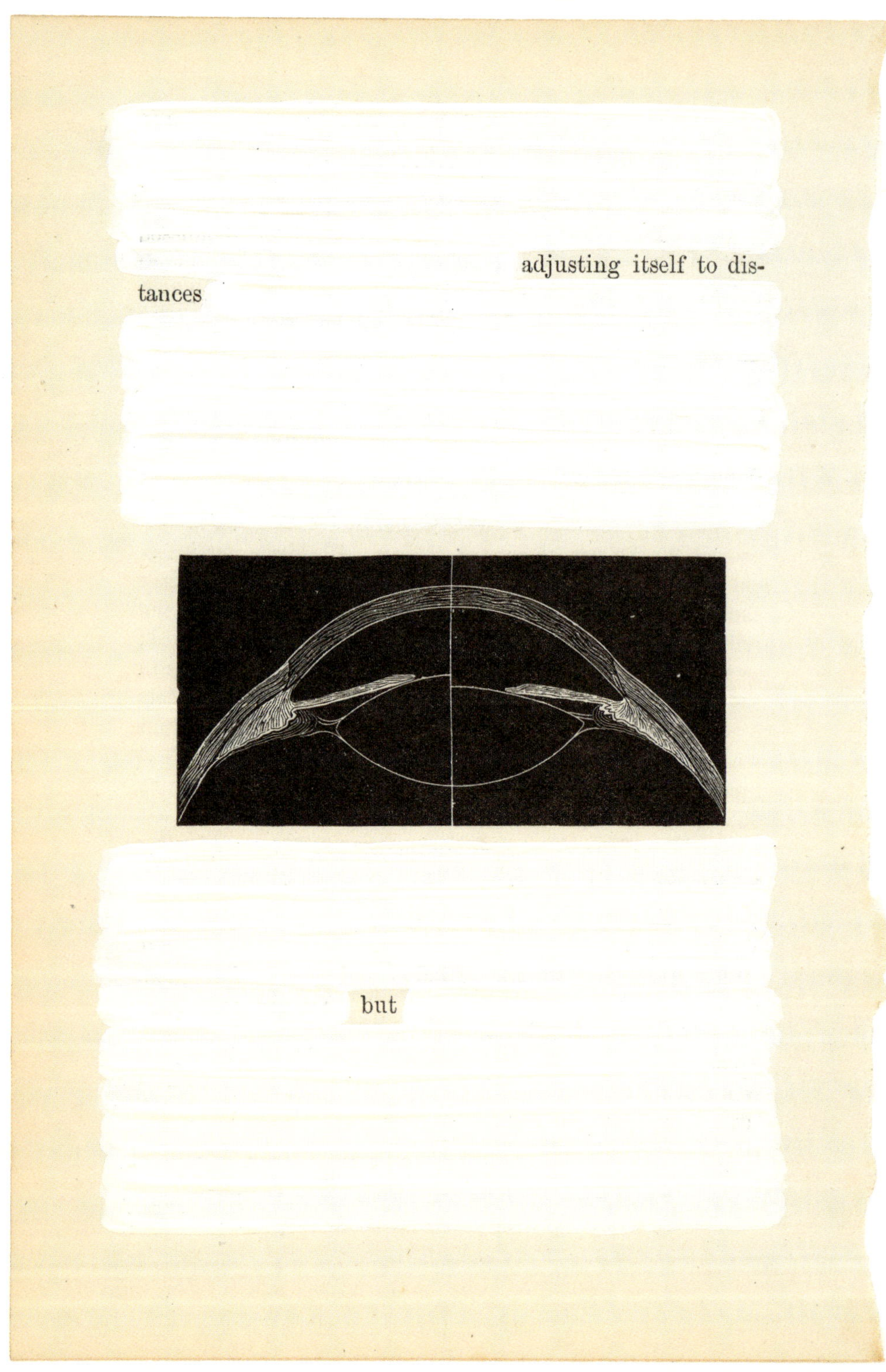

but

may
become
inconvenienced by an overflow upon the face
before it can escape.

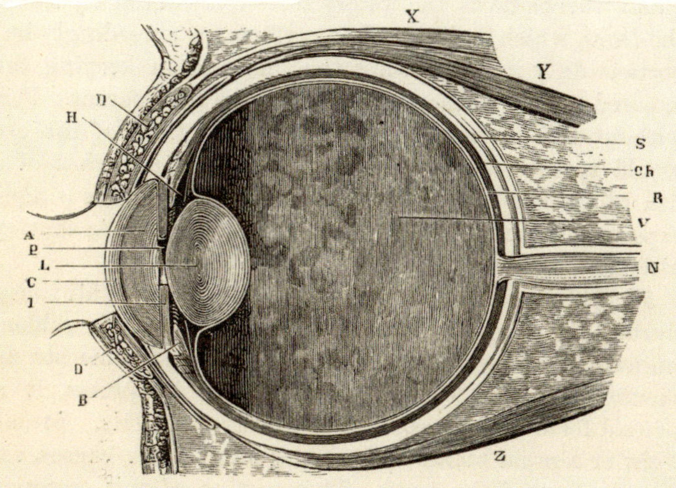

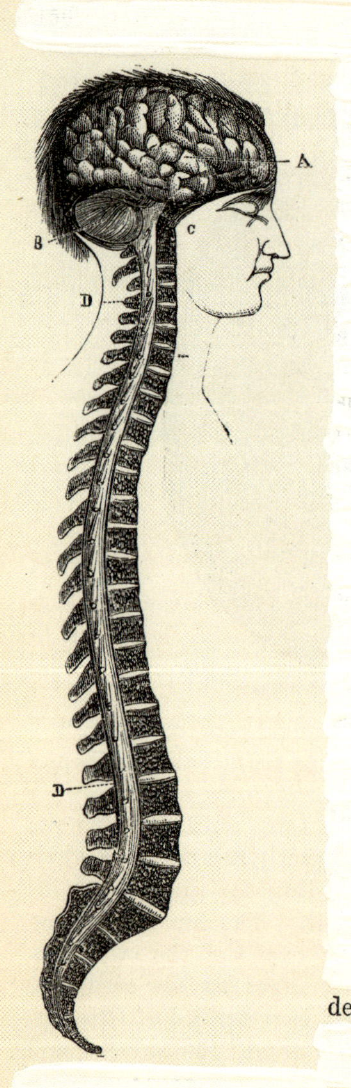

The successive points of
departure
at
regular intervals along
the course of
leaving

by means of branches

the

white variety, or

in glistening, silvery bundles

from one to the other,

one to the other

communicate with the near
and distant regions of the body under their control

like so many

highways over which messages go and
return

A ray of
light, for example, falling

Sta-
tioned at the gate

invisible ene-
mies

grow from the margin

design
their mechanism

scent their prey

find

it is

true

this

bearing

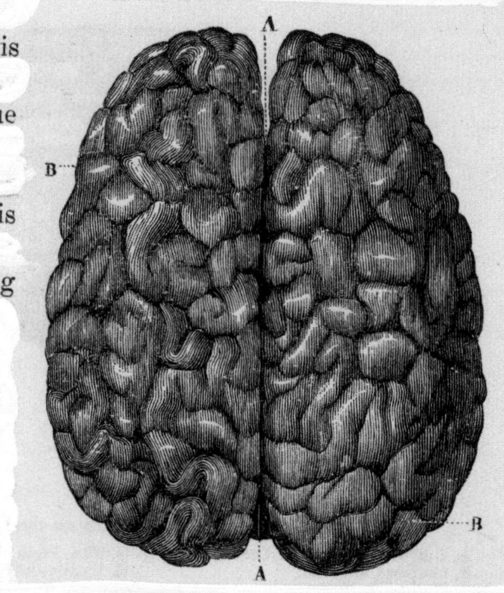

these
furrows
are

divided into hemispheres.
of gray and

gray

around which a delicate network
is arranged

suf-
ficient to maintain

the appetite

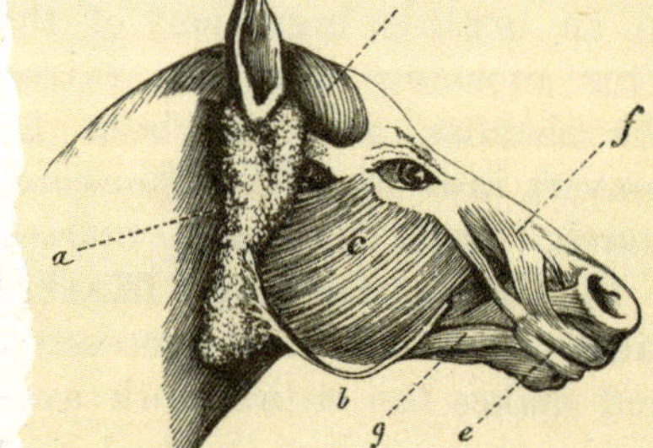

to cleave

and
feed

Walking, sitting, and other acts
of daily life, become automatic:
The dodging motion of the recruit,
when the first cannon ball passes
over his head, the balancing of

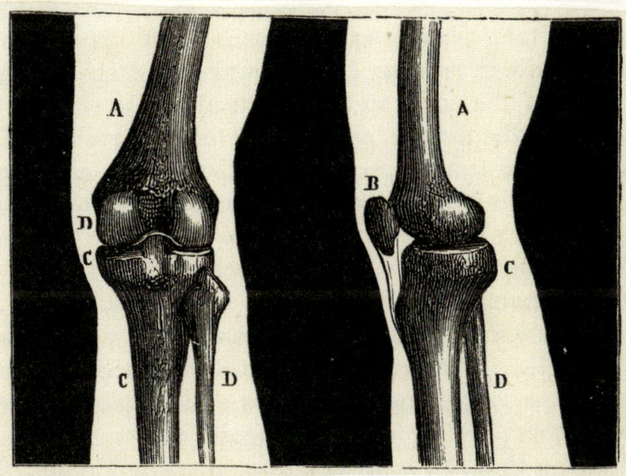

a thousand acts
performed with great precision,
that have been necessary to carry
his body from one point to another,
along a narrow ledge.

By this

beautiful provision

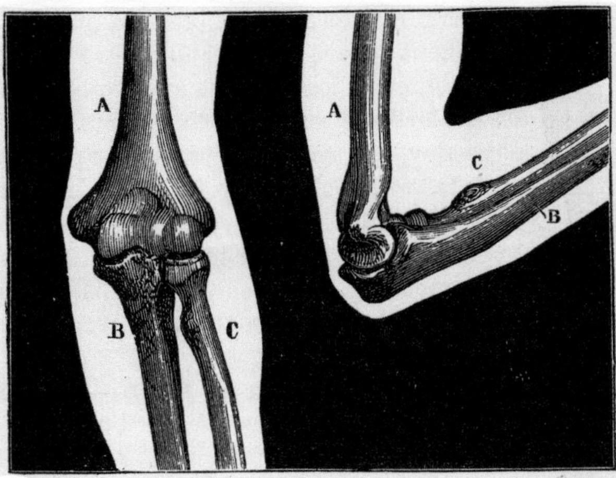

the mind is released

from the

charge of the ordinary —

Laughing,

also sobbing,

from habit: the mind is —

of the —

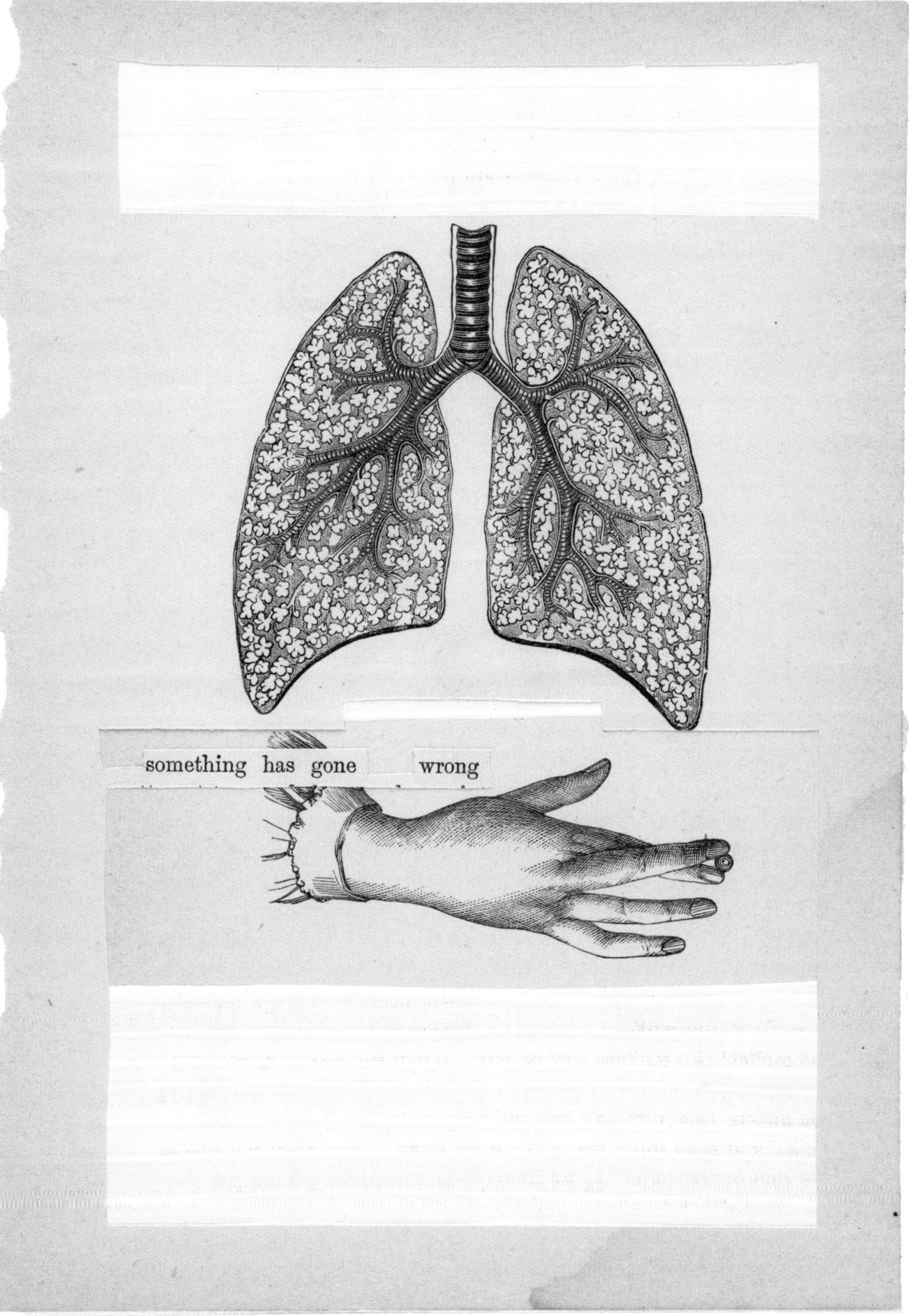
something has gone wrong

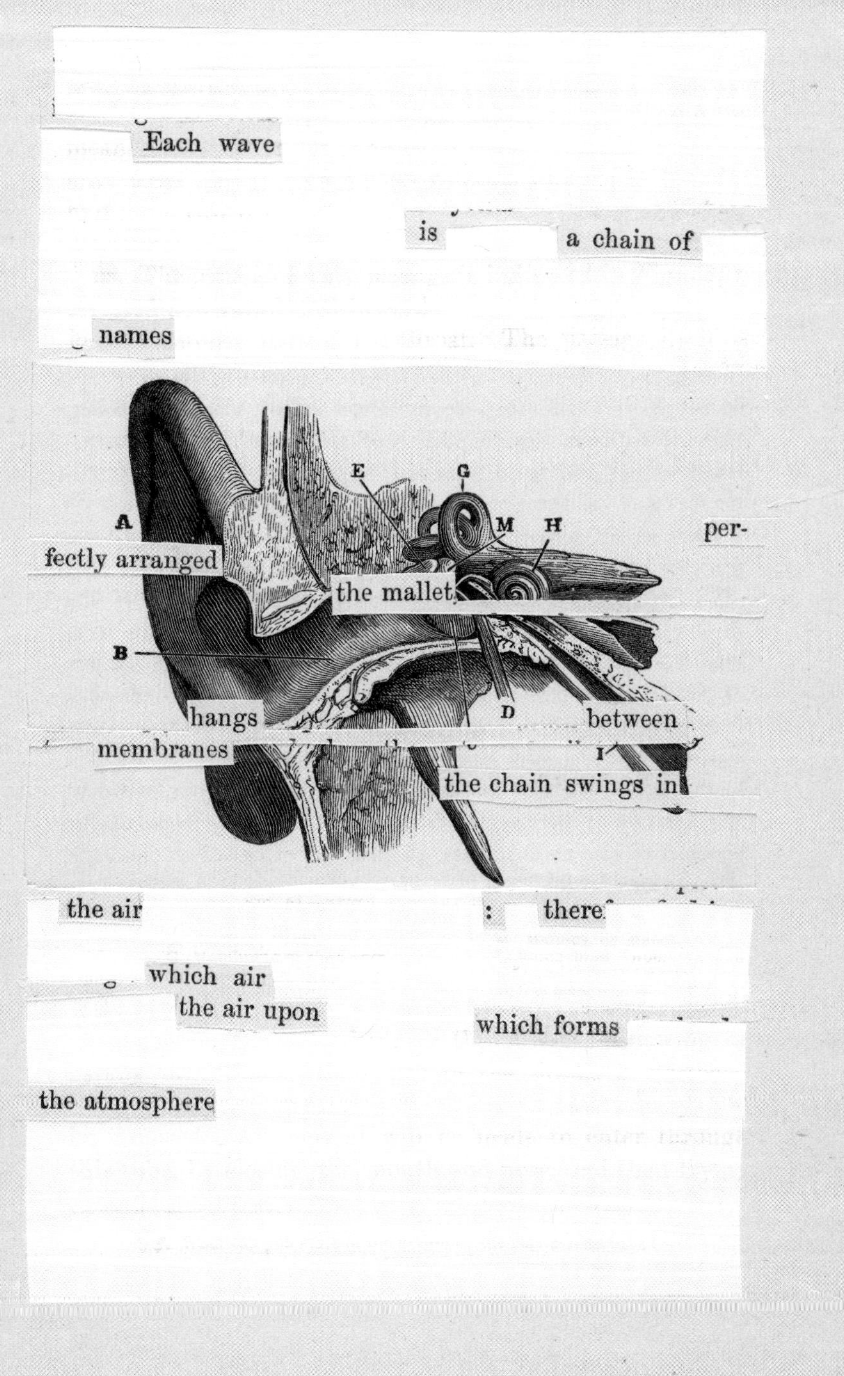
Each wave
is a chain of
names
per-
fectly arranged
the mallet
hangs
between
membranes
the chain swings in
the air
:
theref
which air
the air upon
which forms
the atmosphere
A
B
E
G
M
H
D
I

hollow

chamber,

in which the

remarkable,

liar

floats

sonorous impression

upon a spiral

shelf

destined to be con-

veyed to the

distinguished

office of

echoes

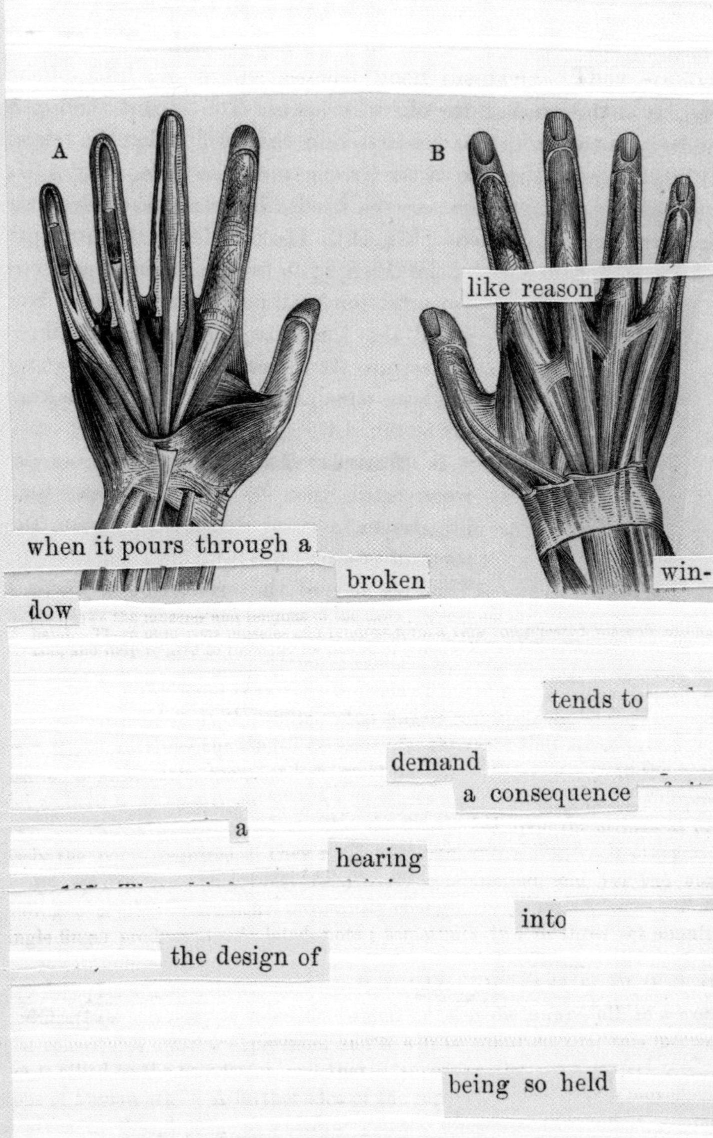
A
B
like reason
when it pours through a
broken
win-
dow
tends to
demand
a consequence
a
hearing
into
the design of
being so held

Through this window, then, the wave
arrives at last

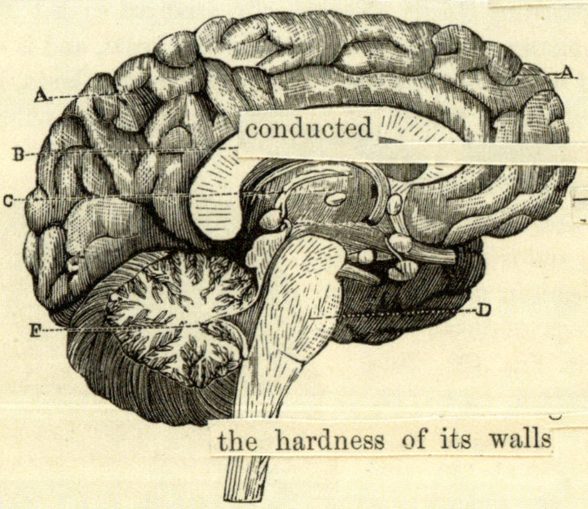

conducted

the hardness of its walls

within
reach

the
cold
familiar
sound

an escape-pipe

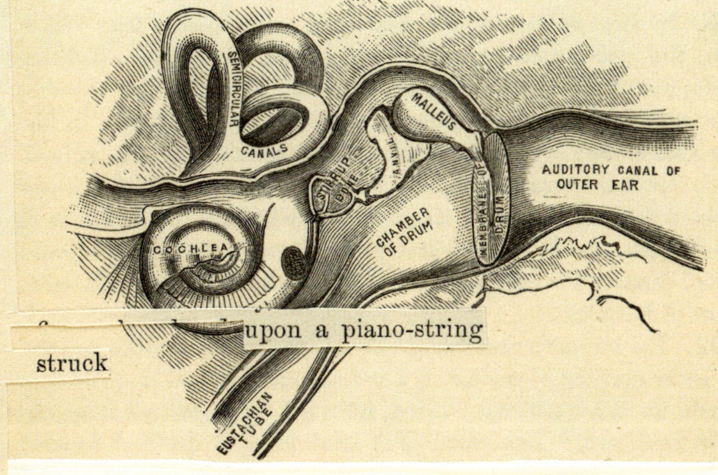

upon a piano-string

struck

ascending as in a balloon

descending as in a diving-bell.

After the battle
crowded into a cavern

during a stormy night,
confined
morning

undergoes
its passage

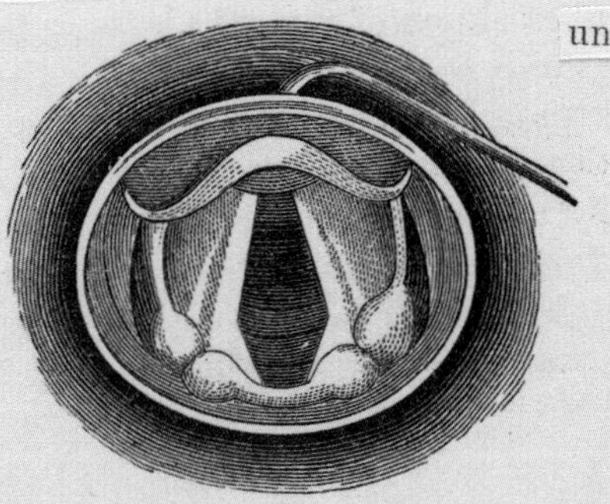

from scarlet to vermilion
brighter than blood

and

the

air, then is a sort of food,

and

borne in mind

the morsel is cut and

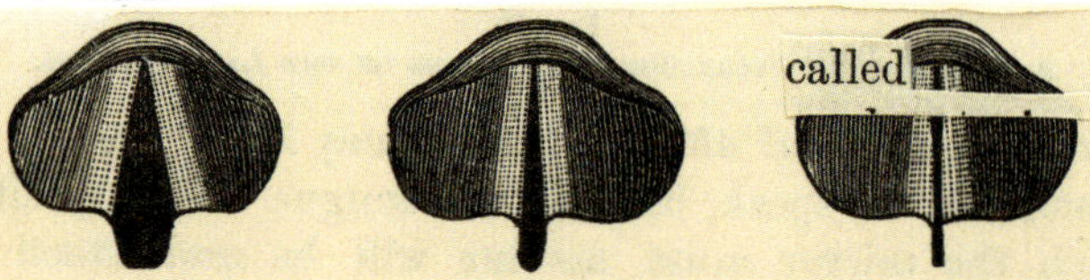

called

near

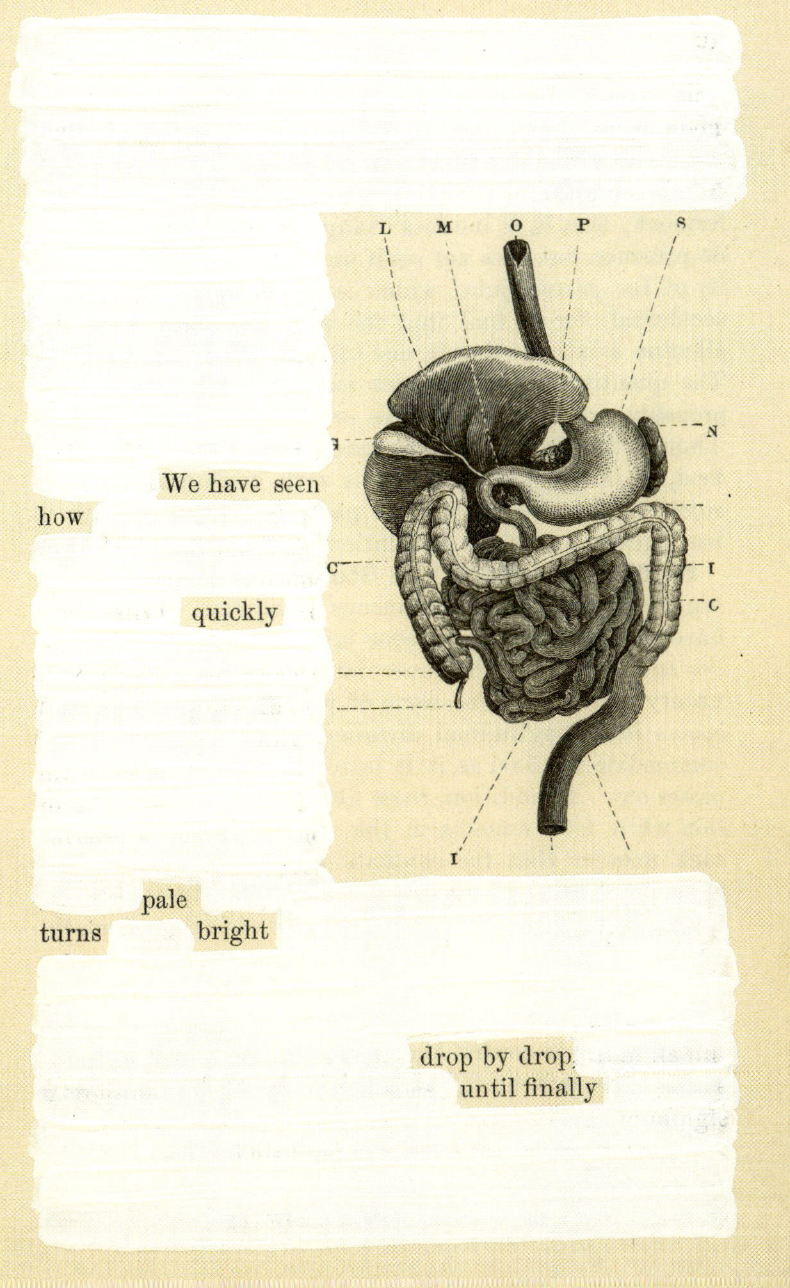
L
M
O
P
S
N
C
I
C
I
We have seen
how
quickly
pale
turns bright
drop by drop
until finally

its wants are met its
losses made good

swallowed
down-

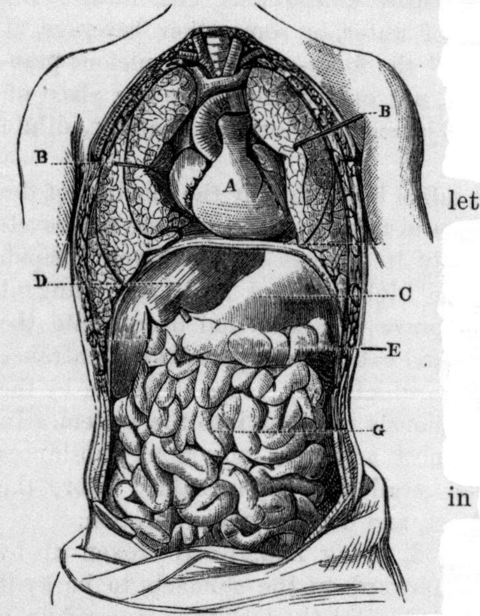

let

in

by

the
gatekeeper which guards the entrance-

in

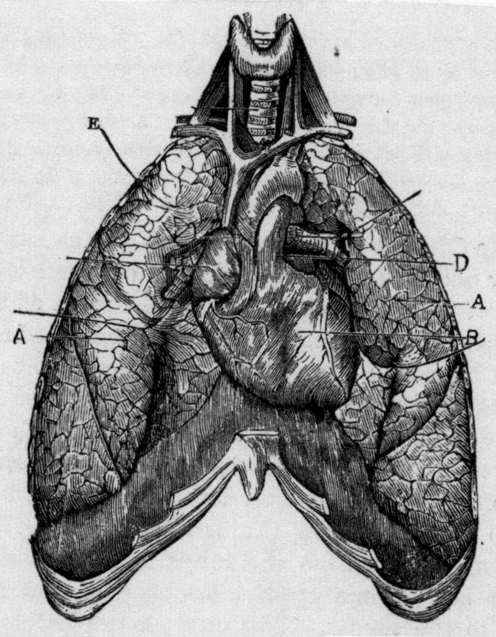

they glide,
one upon the other, with
a secret
to keep:

caught between

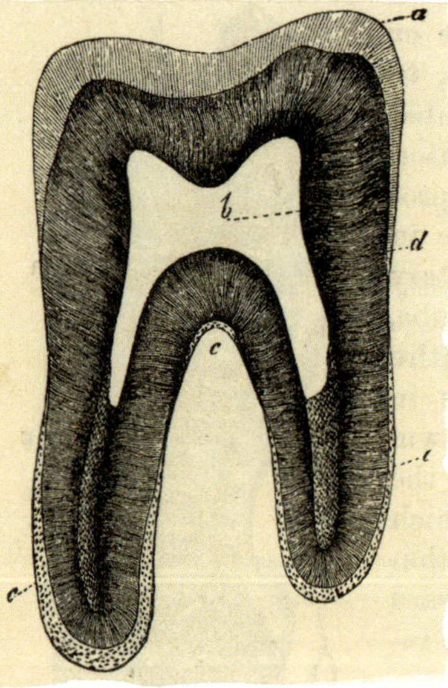

held in place

the body like flint is capable of striking fire

when the body
requires

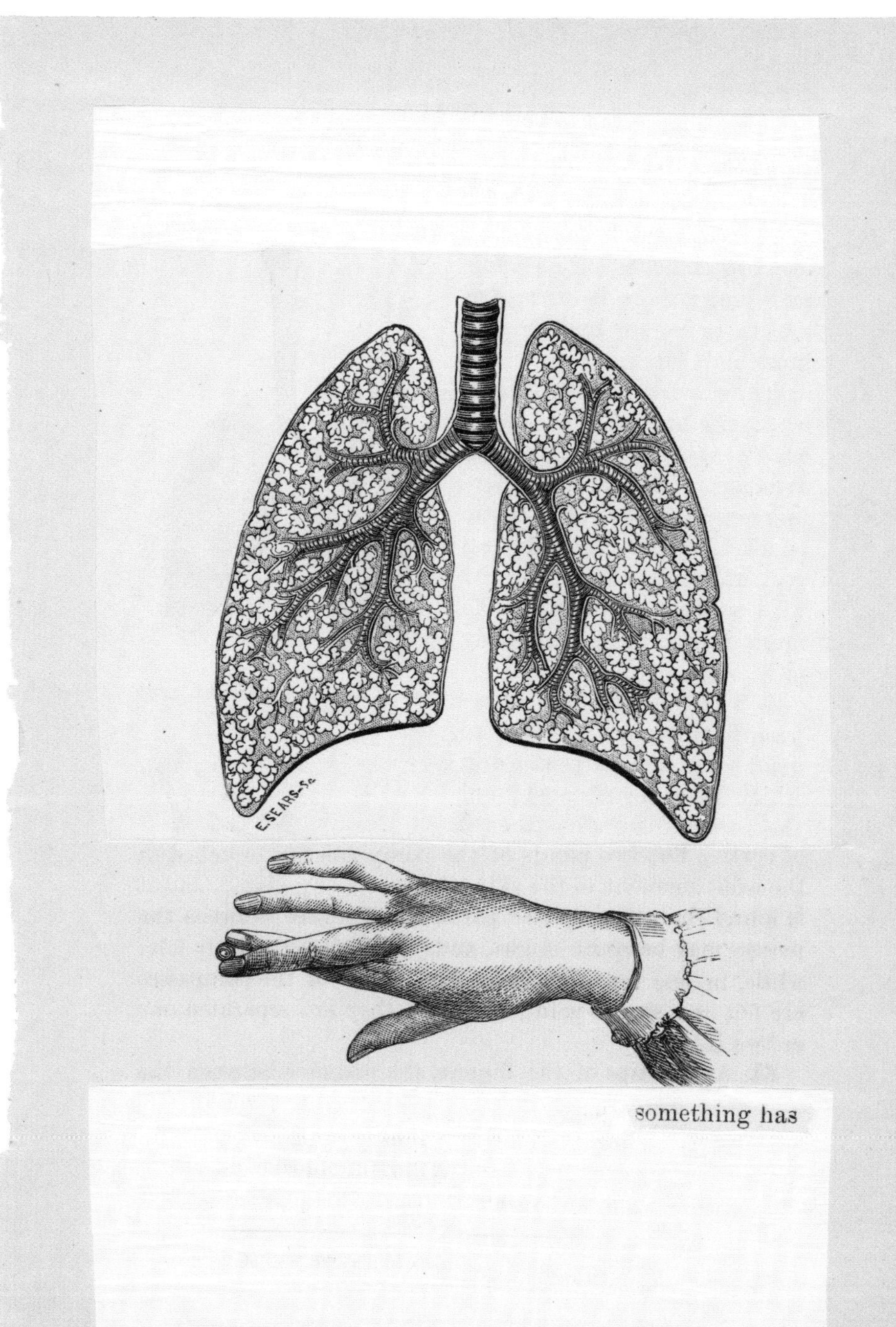
E. SEARS-Sc.
something has

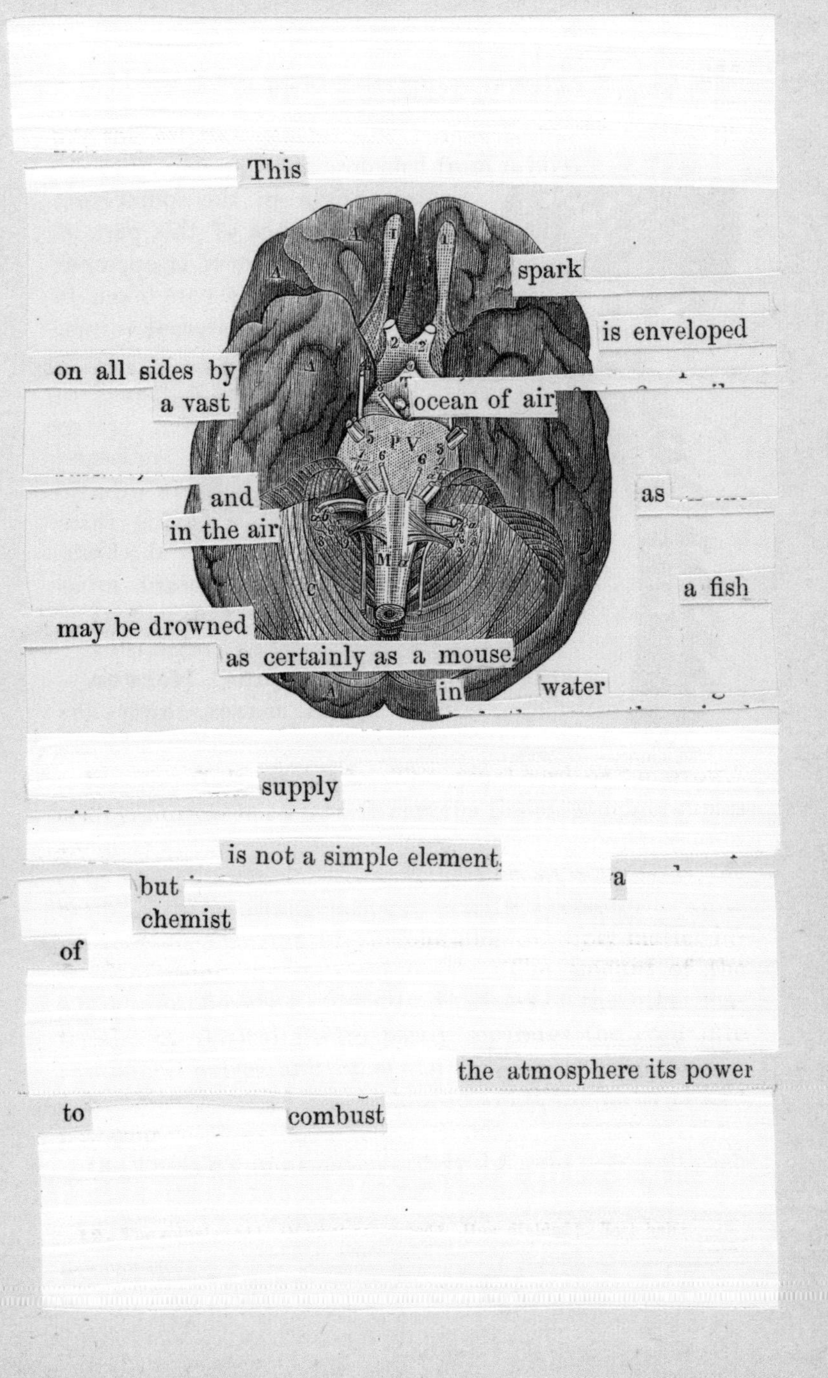

This
spark
is enveloped
on all sides by
a vast ocean of air
and as
in the air
a fish
may be drowned
as certainly as a mouse
in water
supply
is not a simple element,
but a
chemist
of
the atmosphere its power
to combust

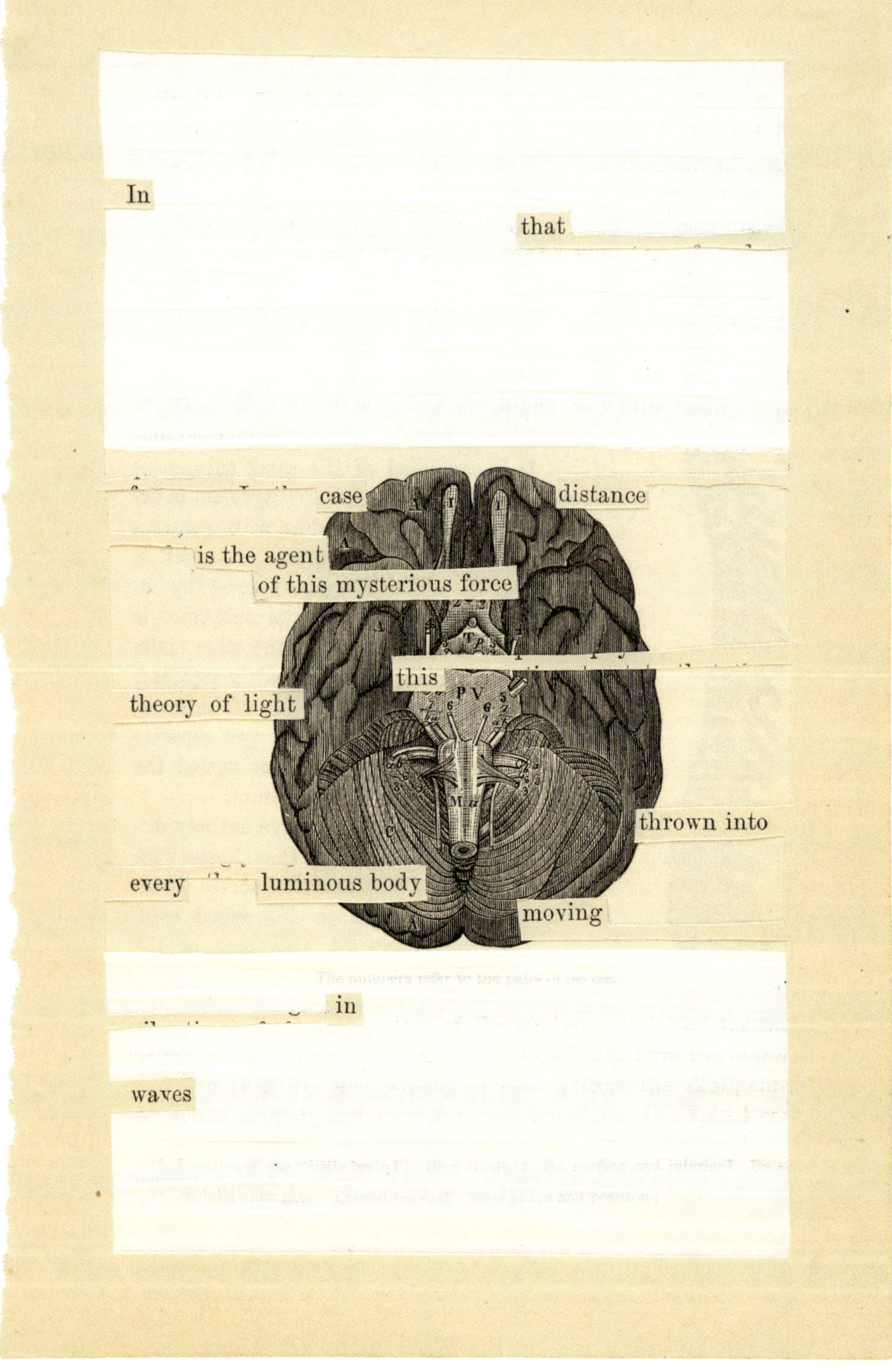
In
that
case
distance
is the agent
of this mysterious force
this
theory of light
thrown into
every
luminous body
moving
in
waves

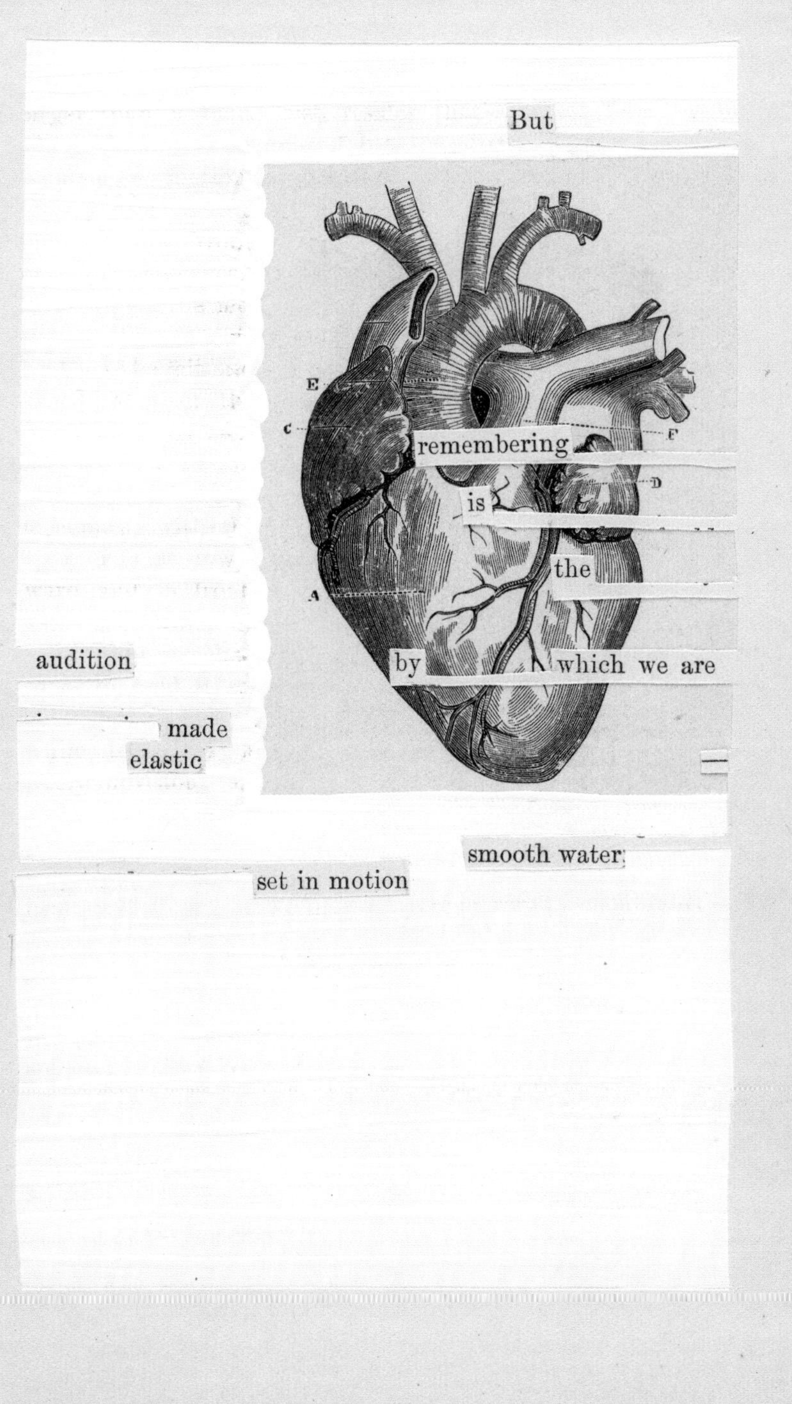
But
E
C
remembering
F
D
is
the
A
audition
by
which we are
made
elastic
smooth water:
set in motion

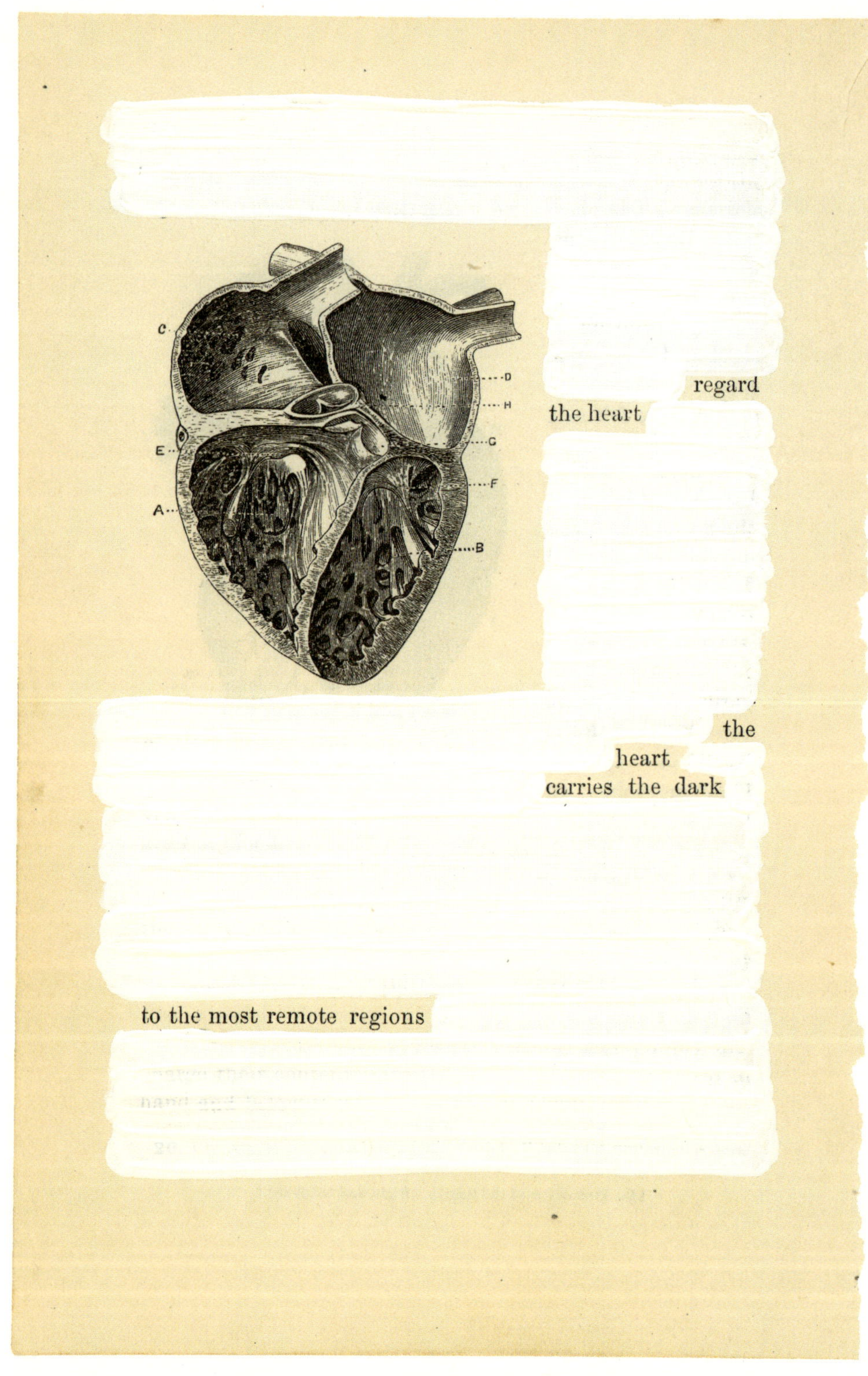
C
D
H
E
G
F
A
B
regard
the heart
the
heart
carries the dark
to the most remote regions

the

dark

that

is dazzling.

the point of entry
all
blind spot.

and

then gradually
the distance from a certain dis-
tance will disappear

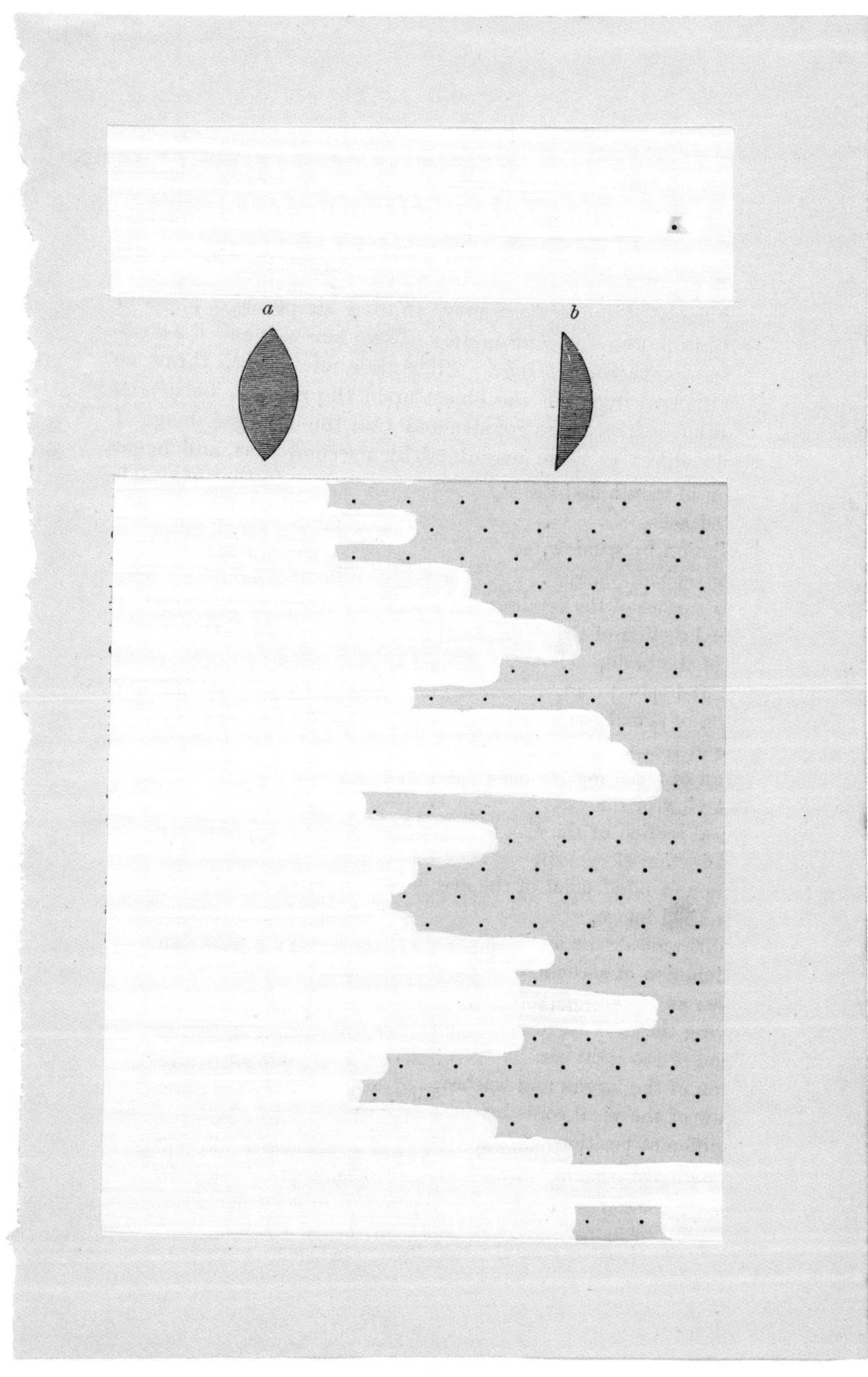
a
b

SOME NOTES ON PROCESS, TIME & DIVINING RODS

Each of the poems making up *Distinguished Office of Echoes* uses a different antique reference book as source text, volumes I found over the course of ten years at favorite used bookstores, in the tucked-away sections where old editions of a certain disposition are shelved. Shelves I visited regularly, like beloved beaches, books I happened upon like tidal treasure. Opening them, I felt the thrum of something revelatory and ecstatic at the intersection of their words and images, in the music they made together and my body perceiving it. I knew immediately that this charge was something I wanted to tap into, the same way I know when I'm hungry that I want to eat.

I ventured into each book briefly, episodically, always at moments of change or loss: during the disorientation of new motherhood; while watching from afar as a climate-driven humanitarian crisis unfolded where I once lived; in the uncanny aftermath of a friend's sudden death. These forays into the source texts offered a lifeline, a means of absorption, contemplation, pursuit. A philosophy of materials and techniques began assembling itself: opaque white watercolor paint *yes,* black ink *no;* blade *yes,* scissors *no;* I'd work in at least two layers, aiming for three, and use nothing longer than a short phrase while avoiding single words. I sensed a place in these books that I needed to go, but it was clear from the start that to discover the red thread I wanted to trace back through a maze toward whatever minotaur I might find would require immersive time.

That time didn't arrive until a dozen years after I had discovered the first book, during the second year of the pandemic while I was trying to recover from a long illness. A leave offered a break from teaching. A rented room provided a makeshift studio. The source texts and my earlier explorations of them gave me a threshold to cross, a realm to enter. Composition became a devotional practice, intensive study a kind of divination. I was the dowser. Attention was my wand of willow tugging in the direction of combinations of words and images, of narrative threads and lyric saliences: the contours of voice, circumstance, lines of inquiry, means of escape or repair.

My first dips into the texts had occurred at moments of fissure, but between March 2021 and January 2022 the experience of making the collages was one of beautiful sustain, a held note. I spent an inordinate amount of time staring at the original source pages before taking the leap of altering them irrevocably, an exorbitant amount of time arranging and rearranging, catching and losing the current that carried me along before I had any idea where I was heading.

The source texts' specialized vocabularies, areas of study, and rhetorical styles were inseparable from their beautiful and beautifully strange images, and from their aging paper and ink. So I dove headlong into a practice defined by direct contact with real materials—by hand, freehand—and by the intimacies and imperfections of embodied experience. In other words, in a landscape saturated with Photoshop, filters, AI, and endless reproduction, this work came from and journeyed into a different place. No spare copies or backups, no *cut, paste, save as,* or *control z,* just the fragile, friable pages of three gorgeous, problematic time-travelers from a long-ago cutting edge of knowledge and production.

My motivation for this approach wasn't nostalgia or critique. It was the gravitational pull of fascination and the productive friction of constraint. It was the draw of a process in which intention was not just informed but transformed by chance and intuition, where I could leave my "I" at the door (or so it seemed). I needed the intimacy and stakes of physical encounter *and* the distance that working with source texts provided. And I needed the gift of collaboration the texts offered across time, a heightened version of the reception, attention, and invention central to any poetry, unfolding in the here-and-now meeting of medium and mind.

So instead of working with notebook, laptop, and Word doc, I tore pages, mixed paint, swapped out X-Acto blades, and held my breath while applying archival glue, relying on an embodied process to draw nearer to the material body of language itself. For months, I didn't sit at a desk, type on a keyboard, or print out drafts. Instead, every surface served a different purpose: desk a gallery wall, counter a workbench laid out with tools. The source texts were like animal presences in the room, shifting their postures as I pulled from them, set them aside, returned, and returned. The room had a cave-like quality; it was best when it rained. Something of the rain's sensibility held even on sunny days. The feeling was one of atmospheric shift, the way light and logic rearrange themselves—rearrange the self—when you swim far enough beneath the water's surface.

Poems begin in the ear for me, but here alongside the ear were the eye and the hand, a visual and tactile listening. Instead of hearing the music of a phrase and following its cadence into something that I could put down on a page, I searched existing pages for those fragmented congregations that seemed to glow or lift or hum. In this material, I found a way to materialize what's always true: that I turn to poetry to tap into fluencies outside of myself, to move beyond what I already know and discover what I don't, to collaborate with language as multisensory medium and ever-evolving meaning-maker.

Within the magnetic field of each source text I found not only a specialized, once-upon-a-time vanguard of science or history, but also a portrait of the pursuit of knowledge itself: how we yearn for and work toward and organize it; how even the best of our knowledge will become outdated, showing itself to be incomplete, perhaps damaging; how a researcher's, writer's, or artist's perspective and voice—the rhythms of their thought—are always present, no matter how objective or removed they might set out to be.

As I engaged with these exquisite repositories of antiquated knowledge, new conversations and alternate findings emerged: between each book's words and images recombined and juxtaposed, and between their acts of research, interpretation, and invention and my own. From an 1865 study of marine invertebrates came an exploration of gathering and dispersal at the moment of death, and of the searching and storytelling that accompany sudden loss. From a 1903 primer on ancient Greek history came a mapping of human versus geologic time, time of war versus time of rivers and seas. From an 1876 medical textbook came a journey into the eerie dislocations of illness, and into reclaiming the voice of the examined. From studying, cutting, collaging, erasing—long-standing compositional techniques in both literary and visual art—came these poems.

SOURCE TEXTS

Seaside Studies in Natural History: Marine Animals of Massachusetts Bay; Radiates; Elizabeth C. Agassiz, Alexander Agassiz; Ticknor and Fields, Boston, 1865.

Greek History for Young Readers; Alice Zimmern; Longmans, Green, and Co., London, New York, and Bombay, 1903.

Hutchison's Physiology and Hygiene: A Treatise on Physiology and Hygiene for Educational Institutions and General Readers; Joseph C. Hutchison; Clark and Maynard, New York, 1876.

A FISH BECOMES A HORSE

Ut pictura poesis.

HORACE

Drop a word in the ocean of meaning and concentric ripples form. To define a single word means to try to catch those ripples. No one's hands are fast enough. Now drop two or three words in at once. Interference patterns form, reinforcing one another here and canceling each other there. To catch the meaning of the words is not to catch the ripples that they cause; it is to catch the interaction of those ripples. This is what it means to listen; this is what it means to read.

ROBERT BRINGHURST

Making a poem is an act of dedicated research and exploration, as the writer builds an expression toward what has not been previously said. It's also an act of participation in the grand conversation that is language. The poem's single voice ripples across time and meets preceding voices, inventing new interactions. As Lisa Olstein reveals in these pages, "remembering / is / the / audition by which we are / made / elastic."

In the prehistoric cave of Pech Merle some 25,000 years ago, a Gravettian artist painted a sturgeon-like fish in red ochre pigment on a rock wall. Deep in the dark, under flickering torchlight, the fish must have come to life as if swimming. Nearby are the images of bison, aurochs, a bear, and a strange human figure pierced through with spear-like lines, as well as the blown ochre handprints of the artists, probably women, who made these images. Nearly 10,000 years later, in this deep and numinous cave, knowledge of which had been passed down over millennia, an artist of the Magdalenian culture built from that original fish image something new and even more stunning. The fish was transformed into a spotted horse, its fin repurposed into an equine back rendered in a nuanced charcoal drawing that used the textures and shapes of the walls to emphasize the horse's muscles, which would have rippled in torchlight.

A studious and focused engagement with inherited material, recast and worked into an alternate way of seeing: this is also Lisa Olstein's project in *Distinguished Office of Echoes.* Olstein gathers language and juxtaposes it with imagery of disembodied viscera, reconfigured maps, and real, floating creatures—medusae, nudibranchs, sea worms and stars—that appear magical. She conjures new life and new territories within her poems.

A lasting poem exists beyond what its words say. The poems in this book, at the nexus of object and speech, are expressions and artifacts full of generative collisions and mystical invitations. Walter Benjamin suggested that writing is a deeply engaged form of reading, and these poem-artworks enact writing and reading simultaneously to create something previously unfelt, unknown. Olstein's process for this work began with an immersion of self in old books, reading, studying, and looking at them as she reflected upon a friend's suicide; as she confronted illness and the body's disorientation; as she sat in bewildered mourning for the world she clearly continues to love. The poems move between reading and writing in search of a greater common ground, gathering a vocabulary of visual imagery and the unspoken. More than a book of lamentations, this is a magical book of grieving, empathy, and recovery.

In *Distinguished Office of Echoes* Olstein turns outward for her interiority, an empathetic act of exploring the intellection and imagination of others as her own journey inward and as a way of participating in global uncertainty. She turns to the original tools of image making within language itself. Her torchlit work creates ripples that expand in search of meaning, connecting with other ripples across time, culture, and different ways of seeing.

Within these pages, history and humanity are collaged. When I first encountered this book, I could not help but consider our communal ecological suicide and the beings that are dying in the oceans and on land. I marveled at how little we yet know of the mutinies of the human body, though we have dissected it for centuries. And I recognized how halting and uncertain language remains—"like reason / when it pours through a / broken win- / dow." Reading this book as we face humanitarian tragedy on a massive yet increasingly familiar scale, I am again transported into the unexpected.

While the book you are holding is singular, it arrived at its form through the fundamental, essential human endeavor of making art. Like the cave painter who turned a fish's fin into a horse's back, Lisa Olstein has gone directly *into* influence.

These poem-collage creations participate in the long history of language's materiality. *Distinguished Office of Echoes* is not merely an archaeological adventure—"in this little book / the heroes are not / some / girls who love the past"—it is part of the embodied present. We follow Olstein in an obsessive pursuit of what she loves and needs to understand; in a deep study of history and biology; in a charged encounter with inherited knowledge; and in a search for the solace that only art can bring.

MICHAEL WIEGERS

ACKNOWLEDGMENTS

Thank you to the John Simon Guggenheim Memorial Foundation for fellowship support that provided time and space crucial to making this work and to the University of Texas at Austin's Office of the Vice President for Research, College of Liberal Arts, and Department of English for research and production support.

Thank you to the friends whose generosity and expertise were vital companions to me while working on this book: Jane Miller, Kris Delmhorst, Deborah Paredez, and Julie Carr for being cherished first readers whose insights and encouragement urged me on; Erika Blumenfeld for helping me see what it was and might become, and for lighting up the path between unruly stack and finished book with her singular brilliance; and Elizabeth McCracken for her genius at editing and friendship.

Thank you to Phil Kovacevich for his all-in collaboration, acumen, and exquisite eye.

Thank you to Michael Wiegers, whose vision and support make so much possible, and to Ryo Yamaguchi, Claretta Holsey, Ashley E. Wynter, and the entire Copper Canyon team for their thoughtful work on this book and their dedication to poets and poetry.

Thank you to my parents, Linda and Michael Olstein, for their unwavering love and support, and for populating my childhood with books, art, music, plants, animals, and seaside creatures. Thank you to David and Toby Goodrich for the life we make together.

ABOUT THE AUTHOR

Lisa Olstein is the author of six poetry collections and two books of nonfiction. Her work has been recognized with a Guggenheim Fellowship, Hayden Carruth Award, Pushcart Prize, Lannan Residency Fellowship, and Sustainable Arts Foundation Promise Award, among other honors. She is a member of the poetry faculty at the University of Texas at Austin where she teaches in the New Writers Project and Michener Center for Writers MFA programs.

ALSO BY LISA OLSTEIN

POETRY

Dream Apartment
Late Empire
Little Stranger
Lost Alphabet
Radio Crackling, Radio Gone

NONFICTION

Climate (with Julie Carr)
Pain Studies

Printed in Canada

Cover art: From *Hutchison's Physiology and Hygiene,* 1876
Cover design: Phil Kovacevich

Copper Canyon Press is in residence at Fort Worden State Park in Port Townsend, Washington, under the auspices of Centrum. Centrum is a gathering place for artists and creative thinkers from around the world, students of all ages and backgrounds, and audiences seeking extraordinary cultural enrichment.

Grateful acknowledgment to Jake Eshelman, photographer; Erika Blumenfeld, artistic advisor; and Phil Kovacevich, art director and book designer.

This book is supported in part by the University of Texas at Austin subvention grant programs of the Office of the Vice President for Research, Scholarship and Creative Endeavors and the College of Liberal Arts.

LIBRARY OF CONGRESS CATALOGING-IN-PUBLICATION DATA
Names: Olstein, Lisa, 1972– author.
Title: Distinguished office of echoes / Lisa Olstein.
Description: Port Townsend, Washington : Copper Canyon Press, 2025. |
Summary: "A collection of poems by Lisa Olstein"— Provided by publisher.
Identifiers: LCCN 2025016623 (print) | LCCN 2025016624 (ebook) |
ISBN 9781556597237 (hardcover) | ISBN 9781619323209 (epub)
Subjects: LCGFT: Poetry.
Classification: LCC PS3615.L78 D57 2025 (print) | LCC PS3615.L78 (ebook) |
DDC 811/.6—dc23/eng/20250512
LC record available at https://lccn.loc.gov/2025016623
LC ebook record available at https://lccn.loc.gov/2025016624

9 8 7 6 5 4 3 2 FIRST PRINTING

COPPER CANYON PRESS
Post Office Box 271
Port Townsend, Washington 98368
www.coppercanyonpress.org

POETS FOR POETRY

Copper Canyon Press poets are at the center of all our efforts as a nonprofit publisher. Poets create the art of our books, and they read and teach the books we publish. Many are also generous donors who believe in financially supporting the vibrant poetry community of Copper Canyon Press. For decades, our poets have quietly donated their royalties, have contributed their time to our fundraising campaigns, and have made personal donations in support of emerging and established poets. Their generosity has encouraged the innovative risk-taking that sustains and furthers the art form.

The donor-poets who have contributed to the Press since 2023 include:

Jonathan Aaron
Pamela Alexander
Kazim Ali
Ellen Bass
Erin Belieu
Mark Bibbins
Linda Bierds
Sherwin Bitsui
Jaswinder Bolina
Marianne Boruch
Laure-Anne Bosselaar
Cyrus Cassells
Peter Cole and Adina Hoffman
Elizabeth J. Coleman
Shangyang Fang
John Freeman
Forrest Gander
Jenny George
Dan Gerber
Jorie Graham
Roger Greenwald
Robert and Carolyn Hedin
Bob Hicok
Ha Jin
The estate of Jaan Kaplinski
Laura Kasischke
Jennifer L. Knox
Ted Kooser
Stephen Kuusisto
Deborah Landau
Sung-Il Lee
Ben Lerner
Dana Levin
Maurice Manning
Heather McHugh
Jane Miller
Roger Mitchell
Lisa Olstein
Gregory Orr
Eric Pankey
Kevin Prufer
Alicia Rabins
Dean Rader
Paisley Rekdal
James Richardson
Alberto Ríos
David Romtvedt
Sarah Ruhl
Kelli Russell Agodon
Natalie Shapero
Arthur Sze
Yuki Tanaka
Elaine Terranova
Chase Twichell
Ocean Vuong
Connie Wanek
Emily Warn

Poetry is vital to language and living. Since 1972, Copper Canyon Press has published extraordinary poetry from around the world to engage the imaginations and intellects of readers, writers, booksellers, librarians, teachers, students, and donors.

We are grateful for the major support provided by:

academy of american poets

TO LEARN MORE ABOUT UNDERWRITING COPPER CANYON PRESS TITLES, PLEASE CALL 360-385-4925 EXT. 105

WE ARE GRATEFUL FOR THE MAJOR SUPPORT PROVIDED BY:

Anonymous

Jill Baker and Jeffrey Bishop

Anne and Geoffrey Barker

Mona Baroudi and Patrick Whitgrove

Lisha Bian

Rick Shinsui Bowles

John Branch

Diana Broze

John R. Cahill

Sarah J. Cavanaugh

Keith Cowan and Linda Walsh

Peter Currie

Geralyn White Dreyfous

The Evans Family

Mimi Gardner Gates

Claire Gribbin

Gull Industries Inc. on behalf of William True

Carolyn and Robert Hedin

David and Jane Hibbard

Bruce S. Kahn

Phil Kovacevich and Eric Wechsler

Eric La Brecque

Maureen Lee and Mark Busto

Ellie Mathews and Carl Youngmann as The North Press

Kathryn O'Driscoll

Petunia Charitable Fund and advisor Elizabeth Hebert

Suzanne Rapp and Mark Hamilton

Adam and Lynn Rauch

Emily and Dan Raymond

Joseph C. Roberts

Cynthia Sears

Kim and Jeff Seely

Tree Swenson

Julia Sze

Donna Wolf

Jamie Wolf

Barbara and Charles Wright

In honor of C.D. Wright from Forrest Gander

Caleb Young as C. Young Creative

The dedicated interns and faithful volunteers of Copper Canyon Press

The pressmark for Copper Canyon Press
suggests entrance, connection, and interaction
while holding at its center
an attentive, dynamic space for poetry.

This book is set in Mrs Eaves.
Book design by Phil Kovacevich.
Printed in Canada on archival-quality paper.